FOB
and
THE HOUSE OF
SLEEPING BEAUTIES

Two Plays by David Henry Hwang

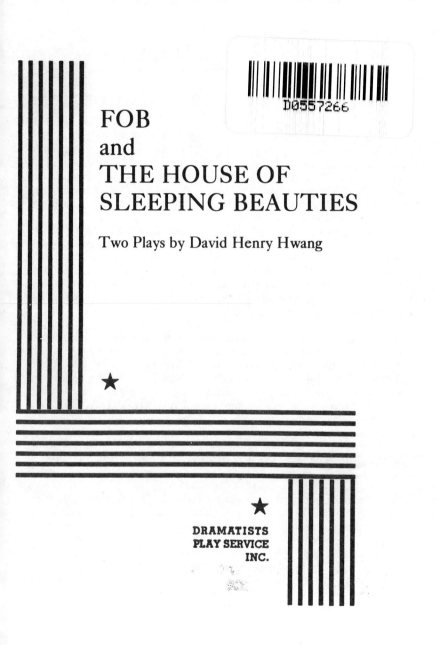

★

★

**DRAMATISTS
PLAY SERVICE
INC.**

D0557266

ABOUT THE AUTHOR

David Henry Hwang is the author of *FOB* (1981 Obie Award, Best New Play; Drama-Logue Award), *The Dance and the Railroad* (Drama Desk Nomination, CINE Golden Eagle Award), *Family Devotions* (Drama Desk Nomination), *The House of Sleeping Beauties,* and *The Sound of a Voice* (Drama-Logue Award), all of which were produced at the New York Shakespeare Festival. *Rich Relations* premiered in 1986 at The Second Stage. *1000 Airplanes on the Roof,* a collaboration with Philip Glass and designer Jerome Sirlin, toured North America, Europe, and Australia in 1988-89. *M. Butterfly* opened on Broadway in 1988 and was honored with the Tony, Drama Desk, Outer Critics Circle, and John Gassner Awards. Mr. Hwang's plays have been anthologized in *Best Plays of 1981-82, Best Short Plays of 1982, New Plays USA 1, Best Short Plays of 1985,* and *Best Plays of 1988-89.* He is the recipient of Guggenheim, Rockefeller, NEA, and NYSCA Fellowships; and serves on the board of the Theatre Communications Group. Mr. Hwang was born in 1957 of immigrant Chinese American parents; he received his undergraduate degree from Stanford University in 1979 and also attended the Yale School of Drama.

CONTENTS

INTRODUCTION

American theater is beginning to discover Americans.

Black theater, women's theater, gay theater, Asian American theater, Hispanic theater—these are more than merely fads' or splinter movements. They are attempts by the American theater to come to grips with the multicultural character of our society, to portray it truthfully. As such, they represent simply the artistic face of what is essentially a political transformation.

By focusing on the smallest thing, we expose the design of the whole. If we neglect some of the communities which make up our society, our perception of the whole becomes a lie. America has traditionally denied the importance of its minorities, and this denial has been reflected in its theater, which has portrayed a relatively homogenous society, with white males as the centers and prime movers. This is ethnic theater—but the theater of only one ethnic group.

The great American temptation is to be suckered into the melting pot. We somehow believe that to be less "ethnic" is to be more human. In fact, the opposite is true: By confronting our ethnicity, we are simply confronting the roots of our humanity. The denial of this truth creates a bizarre world, cut off from the past and alienated from the present, where cosmetic surgeons offer to un-slant Asian eyes and makeup artists work to slant the eyes of Peter Ustinov, 1981's Charlie Chan.

The plays in this volume are my attempt to explore human issues without denying the color of my skin. The playwright Athol Fugard was quoted as saying, "To me, the curse of theater today is generalizing. You need a place, you need the reality first." These plays spring from the world I know best.

These plays also exist as part of the growing Asian American theater movement. Acting remains one of the professions where employment is blatantly denied on the basis of race, and Asian actors who have hoped to play Shakespeare have found themselves on the outskirts of theatrical communities, forced to be mere ethnic color. Asian American theater attempts to counter this denial of our humanity. The reader who appreciates these plays, and especially those who do not, would do well to examine the work of artists such as Philip Kan Gotanda, Momoko Iko, Jessica Hagedorn, Frank Chin, Winston Tong, R.A. Shiomi, and Wakako Yamauchi, in theaters like East West Players (Los Angeles), the Asian American Theatre Company (San Francisco), Pan-Asian Repertory (New York), the Asian Multimedia Center (Seattle), and the Pacific Asian Actors Ensemble (San Diego).

Immigration is making Caucasians an increasingly smaller percentage of this country's population. This demographic trend will necessarily be reflected in the nation's artistic face, and it seems to be a healthy development. In Hawaii, for instance, where Caucasians constitute a plurality rather than a majority, a work of art is not considered somehow "less universal" because its creator is of any particular ethnic group. If this is what the future holds for American theater, we can look forward to a time when no artist will have to hide his or her face in order to work.

In 1979, I directed the first production of my first play, *FOB,* in the lounge of the Okada House dorm at Stanford University. Much has happened since then, and I am grateful to all those who have helped shape these plays, to my family and friends, from whom I am constantly stealing material, and to Joe Papp, who believed in these pieces enough to expose them to a wider audience. It is to Asian American theater people across this nation, however, that I dedicate this volume. I present these plays as an offering, with respect for the past and excitement for our future lives together.

DAVID HENRY HWANG

New York City
May, 1982

8

FOB

For the warriors of my family

PLAYWRIGHTS NOTE

The roots of *FOB* are thoroughly American. The play began when a sketch I was writing about a limousine trip through Westwood, California, was invaded by two figures from American literature: Fa Mu Lan, the girl who takes her father's place in battle, from Maxine Hong Kingston's *The Woman Warrior,* and Gwan Gung, the god of fighters and writers, from Frank Chin's *Gee, Pop!*

This fact testifies to the existence of an Asian American literary tradition. Japanese Americans, for instance, wrote plays in American concentration camps during World War II. Earlier, with the emergence of the railroads, came regular performances of Cantonese operas, featuring Gwan Gung, the adopted god of Chinese America.

FOB was first produced by Nancy Takahashi for the Stanford Asian American Theatre Project. It was performed at Okada House on March 2, 1979, with the following cast:

DALE.................................... Loren Fong
GRACE .... Hope Nakamura
STEVE................................. David Pating

Directed by the author; lights by Roger Tang; sets by George Prince; costumes by Kathy Ko; Randall Tong, assistant director.

The play was then developed at the 1979 O'Neill National Playwrights Conference in Waterford, Connecticut, with the cast of Ernest Abuba, Calvin Jung, and Ginny Yang, directed by Robert Alan Ackerman.

FOB was produced in New York by Joseph Papp at the New York Shakespeare Festival Public Theater, where it opened on June 8, 1980, with the following cast:

DALE.................................... Calvin Jung
GRACE .... Ginny Yang
STEVE.................................... John Lone

On-stage Stage Managers .... Willy Corpus
                                           Tzi Ma
On-stage Musician........................ Lucia Hwong

Directed by Mako; lighting by Victor En Yu Tan; sets by Akira Yoshimura and James E. Mayo; costumes by Susan Hom; choreography by John Lone; music by Lucia Hwong; David Oyama, assistant director.

CHARACTERS
(all in early twenties)

DALE, an American of Chinese descent, second generation.
GRACE, his cousin, a first-generation Chinese American.
STEVE, her friend, A Chinese newcomer.

SCENE

The back room of a small Chinese restaurant in Torrance, California.

TIME

The year 1978. Act I, Scene 1, takes place in the late afternoon. Act I, Scene 2, is a few minutes later. Act II is after dinner.

DEFINITIONS

chong you bing is a type of Chinese pancake, a Northern Chinese appetizer often made with dough and scallions, with a consistency similar to that of *pita* bread.
Gung Gung means "grandfather."
Mei Guo means "beautiful country," a Chinese term for America.
da dao and *mao* are two swords, the traditional weapons of Gwan Gung and Fa Mu Lan, respectively.

FOB

PROLOGUE

Lights up on a blackboard. Enter Dale dressed preppie. The blackboard is the type which can flip around so both sides can be used. He lectures like a university professor, using the board to illustrate his points.

DALE. F-O-B. Fresh Off the Boat. FOB. What words can you think of that characterize the FOB? Clumsy, ugly, greasy FOB. Loud, stupid, four-eyed FOB. Big feet. Horny. Like Lenny in *Of Mice and Men.* Very good. A literary reference. High-water pants. Floods, to be exact. Someone you wouldn't want your sister to marry. If you are a sister, someone you wouldn't want to marry. That assumes we're talking about boy FOBs, of course. But girl FOBs aren't really as ... FOBish. Boy FOBs are the worst, the ... pits. They are the sworn enemies of all ABC—oh, that's "American Born Chinese"—of all ABC girls. Before an ABC girl will be seen on Friday night with a boy FOB in Westwood, she would rather burn off her face. *(He flips around the board. On the other side is written: "1. Where to find FOBs. 2. How to spot a FOB.")* FOBs can be found in great numbers almost anyplace you happen to be, but there are some locations where they cluster in particularly large swarms. Community colleges, Chinese-club discos, Asian sororities, Asian fraternities, Oriental churches, shopping malls, and, of course, BEE GEE concerts. How can you spot a FOB? Look out! If you can't answer that, you might be one. *(He flips back the board, reviews.)* F-O-B. Fresh Off the Boat. FOB. Clumsy, ugly, greasy FOB. Loud, stupid, four-eyed FOB. Big feet. Horny. Like Lenny in *Of Mice and Men.* Floods. Like Lenny in *Of Mice and Men.* F-O-B. Fresh Off the Boat. FOB. *(Lights fade to black. We hear American pop music, preferably in the funk—R&B—disco area.)*

ACT I
Scene 1

The back room of a small Chinese restaurant in Torrance,
California. Single table, with tablecloth; various chairs, sup-
plies. One door leads outside, a back exit, another leads to the
kitchen. Lights up on Grace, at the table. The music is coming
from a small radio. On the table is a small, partially wrapped
box, and a huge blob of discarded Scotch tape. As Grace tries to
wrap the box, we see what has been happening: The tape she's
using is stuck; so, in order to pull it out, she must tug so hard
that an unusable quantity of tape is dispensed. Enter Steve,
from the back door, unnoticed by Grace. He stands, waiting to
catch her eye, tries to speak, but his voice is drowned out by the
music. He is dressed in a stylish summer outfit.

GRACE. Aaaai-ya!

STEVE. Hey! *(No response; he turns off the music.)*

GRACE. Huh? Look. Out of tape.

STEVE. *(In Chinese.)* Yeah.

GRACE. One whole roll. You know how much of it got on here?
Look. That much. That's all.

STEVE. *(In Chinese.)* Yeah. Do you serve *chong you bing* today?

GRACE. *(Picking up box.)* Could've skipped the wrapping paper,
just covered it with tape.

STEVE. *(In Chinese.)* Excuse me!

GRACE. Yeah? *(Pause.)* You wouldn't have any on you, would
ya?

STEVE. *(English from now onward.)* Sorry? No. I don't have *bing.*
I want to buy *bing.*

GRACE. Not *bing!* Tape. Have you got any tape?

STEVE. Tape? Of course I don't have tape.

GRACE. Just checking.

STEVE. Do you have any *bing?* *(Pause.)*

GRACE. Look, we're closed till five...

STEVE. Idiot girl.

GRACE. Why don't you take a menu?

STEVE. I want you to tell me! *(Pause.)*

GRACE. *(Ignoring Steve.)* Working in a Chinese restaurant, you learn to deal with obnoxious customers.

STEVE. Hey! You!

GRACE. If the customer's Chinese, you insult them by giving forks.

STEVE. I said I want you to tell me!

GRACE. If the customer's Anglo, you starve them by not giving forks.

STEVE. You serve *bing or not?*

GRACE. But it's always easy just to dump whatever happens to be in your hands at the moment. *(She sticks the tape blob on Steve's face.)*

STEVE. I suggest you answer my question at once!

GRACE. And I suggest you grab a menu and start doing things for yourself. Look, I'll get you one, even. How's that?

STEVE. I want it from your mouth!

GRACE. Sorry. We don't keep 'em there.

STEVE. If I say they are there, they are there. *(He grabs her box.)*

GRACE. What—What're you doing? Give that back to me! *(They parry around the table.)*

STEVE. Aaaah! Now it's different, isn't it? Now you're listening to me.

GRACE. 'Scuse me, but you really are an asshole, you know that? Who do you think you are?

STEVE. What are you asking me? Who I am?

GRACE. Yes. You take it easy with that, hear?

STEVE. You ask who *I* am?

GRACE. One more second and I'm gonna call the cops.

STEVE. Very well, I will tell you. *(She picks up the phone. He slams it down.)*

STEVE. I said, I'll tell you.

GRACE. If this is how you go around meeting people, I think it's pretty screwed.

STEVE. Silence! I am Gwan Gung! God of warriors, writers, and prostitutes! *(Pause.)*

GRACE. Bullshit!

STEVE. What?

GRACE. Bullshit! Bull-shit! You are not Gwan Gung. And gimme back my box.

STEVE. I am Gwan Gung. Perhaps we should see what you have in here.

GRACE. Don't open that! *(Beat.)* You don't look like Gwan Gung. Gwan Gung is a warrior.

STEVE. I am a warrior!

GRACE. Yeah? Why are you so scrawny, then? You wouldn't last a day in battle.

STEVE. My credit! Many a larger man has been humiliated by the strength in one of my size.

GRACE. Tell me, then. Tell me, if you are Gwan Gung. Tell me of your battles. Of one battle. Of Gwan Gung's favorite battle.

STEVE. Very well. Here is a living memory: One day, Gwan Gung woke up and saw the ring of fire around the sun and decided, "This is a good day to slay villagers." So he got up, washed himself, and looked over a map of the Three Kingdoms to decide where first to go. For those were days of rebellion and falling empires, so opportunity to slay was abundant. But planned slaughter required an order and restraint which soon became tedious. So Gwan Gung decided a change was in order. He called for his tailor, who he asked to make a beautiful blindfold of layered silk, fine enough to be weightless, yet thick enough to blind the wearer completely. The tailor complied, and soon produced a perfect piece of red silk, exactly suited to Gwan Gung's demands. In gratitude, Gwan Gung stayed the tailor's execution sentence. He then put on his blindfold, pulled out his sword, and began passing over the land, swiping at whatever got in his path. You see, Gwan Gung figured there was so much revenge and so much evil in those days that he

16

could slay at random and still stand a good chance of fulfilling justice. This worked very well, until his sword, in its blind fury, hit upon an old and irritable atom bomb. *(Grace catches Steve, takes back the box.)*

GRACE. Ha! Some Gwan Gung you are! Some warrior you are! You can't even protect a tiny box from the grasp of a woman! How could you have shielded your big head in battle?

STEVE. Shield! Shield! I still go to battle!

GRACE. Only your head goes to battle, 'cause only your head is Gwan Gung. *(Pause.)*

STEVE. You made me think of you as a quiet listener. A good trick. What is your name?

GRACE. You can call me "The Woman Who Has Defeated Gwan Gung," if that's really who you are.

STEVE. Very well. But that name will change before long.

GRACE. That story you told—that wasn't a Gwan Gung story.

STEVE. What—you think you know all of my adventures through stories? All the books in the world couldn't record the life of one man, let alone a god. Now—do you serve *bing?*

GRACE. I won the battle; you go look yourself. There.

STEVE. You working here?

GRACE. Part time. It's my father's place. I'm also in school.

STEVE. School? University?

GRACE. Yeah. UCLA.

STEVE. Excellent. I have also come to America for school.

GRACE. Well, what use would Gwan Gung have for school?

STEVE. Wisdom. Wisdom makes a warrior stronger.

GRACE. Pretty good. If you are Gwan Gung, you're not the dumb jock I was expecting. Got a lot to learn about school, though.

STEVE. Expecting? You were expecting me?

GRACE. *(Quickly.)* No, no. I meant, what I expected from the stories.

STEVE. Tell me, how do people think of Gwan Gung in America? Do they shout my name while rushing into battle, or is it too sacred to be used in such ostentatious display?

17

GRACE. Uh—no.

STEVE. No—what? I didn't ask a "no" question.

GRACE. What I mean is, neither. They don't do either of those.

STEVE. Not good. The name of Gwan Gung has been restricted for the use of leaders only?

GRACE. Uh—no. I think you better sit down.

STEVE. This is very scandalous. How are the people to take my strength? Gwan Gung might as well not exist, for all they know.

GRACE. You got it.

STEVE. I got what? You seem to be having trouble making your answers fit my questions.

GRACE. No, I think you're having trouble making your questions fit my answers.

STEVE. What is this nonsense? Speak clearly, or don't speak at all.

GRACE. Speak clearly?

STEVE. Yes. Like a warrior.

GRACE. Well, you see, Gwan Gung, god of warriors, writers, and prostitutes, no one gives a wipe about you 'round here. You're dead. *(Pause.)*

STEVE. You...you make me laugh.

GRACE. You died way back...hell, no one even noticed when you died—that's how bad off your PR was. You died and no one even missed a burp.

STEVE. You lie! The name of Gwan Gung must be feared around the world—you jeopardize your health with such remarks. *(Pause.)* You—you have heard of me, I see. How can you say—?

GRACE. Oh, I just study it a lot—Chinese American history, I mean.

STEVE. Ah. In the schools, in the universities, where new leaders are born, they study my ways.

GRACE. Well, fifteen of us do.

STEVE. Fifteen. Fifteen of the brightest, of the most promising?

GRACE. One wants to be a dental technician.

18

STEVE. A man studies Gwan Gung in order to clean teeth?

GRACE. There's also a middle-aged woman that's kinda bored with her kids.

STEVE. I refuse—I don't believe you—your stories. You're just angry at me for treating you like a servant. You're trying to sap my faith. The people—the people outside—they know me—they know the deeds of Gwan Gung.

GRACE. Check it out yourself.

STEVE. Very well. You will learn—not to test the spirit of Gwan Gung. *(Steve exits. Grace picks up the box. She studies it.)*

GRACE. Fa Mu Lan sits and waits. She learns to be still while the emperors, the dynasties, the foreign lands flow past, unaware of her slender form, thinking it a tree in the woods, a statue to a goddess long abandoned by her people. But Fa Mu Lan, the Woman Warrior, is not ashamed. She knows that the one who can exist without movement while the ages pass is the one to whom no victory can be denied. It is training, to wait. And Fa Mu Lan, the Woman Warrior, must train, for she is no goddess, but girl—girl who takes her father's place in battle. No goddess, but woman—warrior-woman *(She breaks through the wrapping, reaches in, and pulls out another box, beautifully wrapped and ribboned.)* —and ghost. *(She puts the new box on the shelf, goes to the phone, dials.)* Hi, Dale? Hi, this is Grace...Pretty good. How 'bout you?...Good, good. Hey, listen, I'm sorry to ask you at the last minute and everything, but are you doing anything tonight?...Are you sure?...Oh, good. Would you like to go out with me and some of my friends?...Just out to dinner, then maybe we were thinking of going to a movie or something...Oh, good...Are you sure?...Yeah, okay. Um, we're all going to meet at the restaurant...No, *our* restaurant...right—as soon as possible. Okay, good...I'm really glad that you're coming. Sorry it's such short notice. Okay. Bye, now...Huh? Frank? Oh, okay. *(Pause.)* Hi, Frank...Pretty good...Yeah?...No, I don't think so...Yeah...No, I'm sorry, I'd still rather not...I don't want to, okay? Do I have to be any clearer than that?...You are not!...You don't even know when they come—you'd have to lie on those tracks for hours...Forget it, okay?...Look, I'll get you a schedule so you can time it properly...It's not a favor, damn it. Now goodbye! *(She hangs up.)* Jesus! *(Steve enters.)*

STEVE. Buncha weak boys, what do they know? One man— ChinaMan—wearing a leisure suit—green! I ask him, "You know Gwan Gung?" He says, "Hong Kong?" I say, "No, no. Gwan Gung." He says, "Yeah. They got sixty thousand people living on four acres. Went there last year." I say, "No, no. Gwan Gung." He says, "Ooooh! Gwan Gung?" I say, "Yes, yes, Gwan Gung." He says, "I never been there before."

GRACE. See? Even if you didn't die—who cares?

STEVE. Another kid—blue jeans and a T-shirt—I ask him, does he know Gwan Gung? He says, he doesn't need it, he knows Jesus Christ. What city is this now?

GRACE. Los Angeles.

STEVE. This isn't the only place where a new ChinaMan can land, is it?

GRACE. I guess a lot go to San Francisco.

STEVE. Good. This place got a bunch of weirdos around here.

GRACE. Yeah.

STEVE. They could never be followers of Gwan Gung. All who follow me must be loyal and righteous.

GRACE. Maybe you should try some other state.

STEVE. Huh? What you say?

GRACE. Never mind. You'll get used to it—like the rest of us. *(Pause. Steve begins laughing.)*

STEVE. You are a very clever woman.

GRACE. Just average.

STEVE. No. You do a good job to make it seem like Gwan Gung has no followers here. At the university, what do you study?

GRACE. Journalism.

STEVE. Journalism—you are a writer, then?

GRACE. Of a sort.

STEVE. Very good. You are close to Gwan Gung's heart.

GRACE. As close as I'm gonna get.

STEVE. I would like to go out tonight with you.

GRACE. I knew it. Look, I've heard a lot of lines before, and yours is very creative, but...

STEVE. I will take you out.

GRACE. You will, huh?

STEVE. I do so because I find you worthy to be favored.

GRACE. You're starting to sound like any other guy now.

STEVE. I'm sorry?

GRACE. Look—if you're going to have any kinds of relationships with women in this country, you better learn to give us some respect.

STEVE. Respect? I give respect.

GRACE. The pushy, aggressive type is out, understand?

STEVE. Taking you out is among my highest tokens of respect.

GRACE. Oh, c'mon—they don't even say that in Hong Kong.

STEVE. You are being asked out by Gwan Gung!

GRACE. I told you, you're too wimpy to be Gwan Gung. And even if you were, you'd have to wait your turn in line.

STEVE. What?

GRACE. I already have something for tonight. My cousin and I are having dinner.

STEVE. You would turn down Gwan Gung for your cousin?

GRACE. Well, he has a X-1/9. *(Pause.)*

STEVE. What has happened?

GRACE. Look—I tell you what. If you take both of us out, then it'll be okay, all right?

STEVE. I don't want to go out with your cousin!

GRACE. Well, sorry. It's part of the deal.

STEVE. Deal? What deals? Why am I made part of these deals?

GRACE. 'Cause you're in the U.S. in 1980, just like the rest of us. Now quit complaining. Will you take it or not? *(Pause.)*

STEVE. Gwan Gung...bows to no one's terms but his own.

GRACE. Fine. Why don't you go down the street to Imperial Dragon Restaurant and see if they have *bing?*

STEVE. Do you have *bing?*

GRACE. See for yourself. *(She hands him a menu. He exits. Grace moves with the box.)* Fa Mu Lan stood in the center of the village and turned round and round as the bits of fingers, the tips of tongues, the arms, the legs, the peeled skulls, the torn maidenheads, all whirled by. She pulled the loose gown closer to her body, stepped over the torsos, in search of the one of her family who might still be alive. Reaching the house that was once her home, crushing bones in her haste, only to find the doorway covered with the stretched and dried skin of that which was once her father. Climbing through an open window, noticing the shiny black thousand-day-old egg still floating in the shiny black sauce. Finding her sister tied spread-eagle on the mat, finding her mother in the basket in pieces, finding her brother nowhere. The Woman Warrior went to the mirror, which had stayed unbroken, and let her gown come loose and drop to the ground. She turned and studied the ideographs that had long ago been carved into the flesh of her young back...Carved by her mother, who lay carved in the basket. *(Dale enters, approaches Grace.)* She ran her fingers over the skin and felt the ridges where there had been pain. *(Dale is behind Grace.)* But now they were firm and hard. *(Dale touches Grace, who reacts by swinging around and knocking him to the ground. Only after he is down does she see his face.)* Dale! Shit! I'm sorry. I didn't...!

DALE. *(Groggy.)* Am I late?

GRACE. I didn't know it was you, Dale.

DALE. Yeah. Well, I didn't announce myself.

GRACE. You shouldn't just come in here like that.

DALE. You're right. Never again.

GRACE. I mean, you should've yelled from the dining room.

DALE. Dangerous neighborhood, huh?

GRACE. I'm so sorry. Really.

DALE. Yeah. Uh—where're your other friends? They on the floor around here too?

GRACE. No. Uh—this is really bad, Dale. I'm really sorry.

DALE. What?—you can't make it after all?

GRACE. No, I can make it. It's just that...

DALE. They can't make it? Okay, so it'll just be us. That's cool.

GRACE. Well, not quite us.

DALE. Oh.

GRACE. See, what happened is—You know my friend, Judy?

DALE. Uh—no.

GRACE. Well, she was gonna come with us—with me and this guy I know—his name is...Steve.

DALE. Oh, he's with you, right?

GRACE. Well, sort of. So since she was gonna come, I thought you should come too.

DALE. To even out the couples?

GRACE. But now my friend Judy, she decided she had too much work to do, so...oh it's all messed up.

DALE. Well, that's okay. I can go home—or I can go with you, if this guy Steve doesn't mind. Where is he, anyway?

GRACE. I guess he's late. You know, he just came to this country.

DALE. Oh yeah? How'd you meet him?

GRACE. At a Chinese dance at U.C.L.A.

DALE. Hmmmmm. Some of those FOBs get moving pretty fast. *(Grace glares.)* Oh. Is he...nice?

GRACE. He's okay. I don't know him that well. You know, I'm really sorry.

DALE. Hey, I said it was okay. Jesus, it's not like you hurt me or anything.

GRACE. For that, too.

DALE. Look—*(He hits himself.)* No pain!

GRACE. What I meant was, I'm sorry tonight's got so messed up.

DALE. Oh, it's okay. I wasn't doing anything anyway.

GRACE. I know, but still...*(Silence.)*

DALE. Hey, that Frank is a joke, huh?

GRACE. Yeah. He's kind of a pain.

DALE. Yeah. What an asshole to call my friend.

GRACE. Did you hear him on the phone?

DALE. Yeah, all that railroad stuff?

GRACE. It was real dumb.

DALE. Dumb? He's dumb. He's doing it right now.

GRACE. Huh? Are you serious?

DALE. Yeah. I'm tempted to tie him down so, for once in his life, he won't screw something up.

GRACE. You're kidding!

DALE. Huh? Yeah, sure I'm kidding. Who would I go bowling with?

GRACE. No, I mean about him actually going out there—is that true?

DALE. Yeah—he's lying there. You know, right on Torrance Boulevard?

GRACE. No!

DALE. Yeah!

GRACE. But what if a train really comes?

DALE. I dunno. I guess he'll get up.

GRACE. I don't believe it!

DALE. Unless he's fallen asleep by that time or something.

GRACE. He's crazy.

DALE. Which is a real possibility for Frank, he's such a bore anyway.

GRACE. He's weird.

DALE. No, he just thinks he's in love with you.

GRACE. Is he?

DALE. I dunno. We'll see when the train comes.

GRACE. Do you think we should do something?

DALE. What?—You're not gonna fall for the twerp, are you?

GRACE. Well, no, but...

DALE. He's stupid—and ugly, to boot.

GRACE. ...but staying on the tracks is kinda dangerous.

DALE. Let him. Teach him a lesson.

GRACE. You serious?

DALE. *(Moving closer to Grace.)* Not to fool with my cousin. *(He strokes her hair. They freeze in place, but his arm continues to stroke. Steve enters, oblivious of Dale and Grace, who do not respond to him. He speaks to the audience as if it were a panel of judges.)*

STEVE. No! Please! Listen to me! This is fifth time I come here.

I tell you both my parents, I tell you their parents, I tell you their parents' parents and who was adopted great-granduncle. I tell you how many beggars in home town and name of their blind dogs. I tell you number of steps from my front door to temple, to well, to governor house, to fields, to whorehouse, to fifth cousin inn, to eighth neighbor toilet—you ask only: What for am I in whorehouse? I tell north, south, northeast, southwest, west, east, north-northeast, south-southwest, east-eastsouth—Why will you not let me enter in America? I come here five times—I raise lifetime fortune five times. Five times, I first come here, you say to me I am illegal, you return me on boat to fathers and uncles with no gold, no treasure, no fortune, no rice. I only want to come to America—come to "Mountain of Gold." And I hate Mountain and I hate America and I hate you! *(Pause.)* But this year you call 1914—very bad for China. *(Pause; light shift. Grace and Dale become mobile and aware of Steve's presence.)*

GRACE. Oh! Steve, this is Dale, my cousin. Dale, Steve.

DALE. Hey, nice to meet...

STEVE. *(Now speaking with Chinese accent.)* Hello. Thank you. I am fine. *(Pause.)*

DALE. Uh, yeah. Me too. So, you just got here, huh? What'cha think? *(Steve smiles and nods, Dale smiles and nods; Steve laughs, Dale laughs; Steve hits Dale on the shoulder. They laugh some more. They stop laughing.)* Oh. Uh—good. *(Pause.)* Well, it looks like it's just gonna be the three of us, right? *(To Grace.)* Where you wanna go?

GRACE. I think Steve's already taken care of that. Right, Steve?

STEVE. Excuse?

GRACE. You made reservations at a restaurant?

STEVE. Oh, reservations. Yes, yes.

DALE. Oh, okay. That limits the possibilities. Guess we're going to Chinatown or something, right?

GRACE. *(To Steve.)* Where is the restaurant?

STEVE. Oh. The restaurant is a French restaurant. Los Angeles downtown.

DALE. Oh, we're going to a Western place? *(To Grace.)* Are you sure he made reservations?

GRACE. We'll see.

DALE. Well, I'll get my car.

GRACE. Okay.

STEVE. No!

DALE. Huh?

STEVE. Please—allow me to provide car.

DALE. Oh. You wanna drive.

STEVE. Yes. I have car.

DALE. Look—why don't you let me drive? You've got enough to do without worrying about—you know—how to get around L.A., read the stop signs, all that.

STEVE. Please—allow me to provide car. No problem.

DALE. Well, let's ask Grace, okay? *(To Grace.)* Grace, who do you think should drive?

GRACE. I don't really care. Why don't you two figure it out? But let's hurry, okay? We open pretty soon.

DALE. *(To Steve.)* Look—you had to pick the restaurant we're going to, so the least I can do is drive.

STEVE. Uh, your car—how many people sit in it?

DALE. Well, it depends. Right now, none.

GRACE. *(To Dale.)* He's got a point. Your car only seats two.

DALE. He can sit in the back. There's space there. I've fit luggage in it before.

GRACE. *(To Steve.)* You want to sit in back?

STEVE. I sit—where?

DALE. Really big suitcases.

GRACE. Back of his car.

STEVE. X-1/9? Aaaaai-ya!

DALE. X-1/9?

STEVE. No deal!

DALE. How'd he know that? How'd he know what I drive?

STEVE. Please. Use my car. Is...big.

DALE. Yeah? well, how much room you got? *(Pause; slower.)* How-big-your-car-is?

STEVE. Huh?

26

DALE. Your car—how is big?

GRACE. How big is your car?

STEVE. Oh! You go see.

DALE. 'Cause if it's like, a Pinto or something, it's not that much of a difference.

STEVE. Big and black. Outside.

GRACE. Let's hurry.

DALE. Sure, sure. *(Exits.)*

GRACE. What you up to, anyway?

STEVE. *(Dropping accent.)* Gwan Gung will not go into battle without equipment worthy of his position.

GRACE. Position? You came back, didn't you? What does that make you?

DALE. *(Entering.)* Okay. There's only one black car out there—

STEVE. Black car is mine.

DALE. —and that's a Fleetwood limo. Now, you're not gonna tell me that's his.

STEVE. Cadillac. Cadillac is mine.

DALE. Limousine...Limousine is yours?

STEVE. Yes, yes. Limousine. *(Pause.)*

DALE. *(To Grace.)* You wanna ride in the black thing? People will think we're dead.

GRACE. It does have more room.

DALE. Well, it has to. It's built for passengers who can't bend.

GRACE. And the driver *is* expensive.

DALE. He could go home—save all that money.

GRACE. Well, I don't know. You decide.

DALE. *(To Steve.)* Look, we take my car, savvy?

STEVE. Please—drive my car.

DALE. I'm not trying to be unreasonable or anything.

STEVE. My car—just outside.

DALE. I know where it is, I just don't know why it is.

GRACE. Steve's father manufactures souvenirs in Hong Kong.

DALE. *(To Steve.)* Oh, and that's how you manage that out there, huh?—from thousands of aluminum Buddhas and striptease pens.

GRACE. Well, he can't drive and he has the money—

DALE. *(To Grace.)* I mean, wouldn't you just feel filthy?

GRACE. —so it's easier for him.

DALE. Getting out of a limo in the middle of Westwood? People staring, thinking we're from 'SC? Wouldn't you feel like dirt?

GRACE. It doesn't matter either way to me. *(Pause.)*

DALE. Where's your social conscience?

GRACE. Look—I have an idea. Why don't we just stay here.

STEVE. We stay here to eat?

GRACE. No one from the restaurant will bother us, and we can bring stuff in from the kitchen.

STEVE. I ask you to go out.

DALE. Look, Grace, I can't put ya out like that.

GRACE. *(To Dale.)* It's no problem, really. It should be fun. *(To Steve.)* Since there are three of us—

DALE. Fun?

GRACE. *(To Steve.)* —it is easier to eat here.

DALE. How can it be fun? It's cheaper.

STEVE. Does not seem right.

GRACE. I mean, unless our restaurant isn't nice enough.

DALE. No, no—that's not it.

STEVE. *(Watching Dale.)* No—this place, very nice.

GRACE. Are you sure?

DALE. Yeah. Sure.

STEVE. *(Ditto.)* Yeah. Sure.

DALE. Do you have...uh—those *burrito* things?

GRACE. *Moo-shoo?*

DALE. Yeah, that.

GRACE. Yeah.

DALE. And black mushrooms.

GRACE. Sure.

DALE. And sea cucumber?

STEVE. Do you have *bing? (Pause.)*

GRACE. Look, Dad and Russ and some of the others are gonna

be setting up pretty soon, so let's get our place ready, okay?

DALE. Okay. Need any help?

GRACE. Well, yeah. That's what I just said.

DALE. Oh, right. I thought maybe you were just being polite.

GRACE. Yeah. Meet me in the kitchen.

DALE. Are you sure your dad won't mind?

GRACE. What?

DALE. Cooking for us.

GRACE. Oh, it's okay. He'll cook for anybody. *(Exits. Silence.)*

DALE. So, how do you like America?

STEVE. Very nice.

DALE. "Very nice." Good, colorful Hong Kong English. English—how much of it you got down, anyway?

STEVE. Please repeat?

DALE. English—you speak how much?

STEVE. Oh—very little.

DALE. Honest. *(Pause.)* You feel like you're an American? Don't tell me. Lemme guess. Your father. *(He switches into a mock Hong Kong accent.)* Your fad-dah tink he sending you here so you get yo' M.B.A., den go back and covuh da world wit' trinkets and beads. Diversify. Franchise. Sell—ah—Hong Kong X-Ray glasses at tourist shop at Buckingham Palace. You know—ah—"See da Queen"? *(Switches back.)* He's hoping your American education's gonna create an empire of defective goods and breakable merchandise. Like those little cameras with the slides inside? I bought one at Disneyland once and it ended up having pictures of Hong Kong in it. You know how shitty it is to expect the Magic Kingdom and wind up with the skyline of Kowloon? Part of your dad's plan, I'm sure. But you're gonna double-cross him. Coming to America, you're gonna jump the boat. You're gonna decide you like us. Yeah—you're gonna like having fifteen theaters in three blocks, you're gonna like West Hollywood and Newport Beach. You're gonna decide to become an American. Yeah, don't deny it—it happens to the best of us. You can't hold out—you're no different. You won't even know it's coming before it has you. Before you're trying

29

real hard to be just like the rest of us—go dinner, go movie, go motel, bang-bang. And when your father writes you that do-it-yourself acupuncture sales are down, you'll throw that letter in the basket and burn it in your brain. And you'll write that you're gonna live in Monterey Park a few years before going back home—and you'll get your green card—and you'll build up a nice little stock-broker's business and have a few American kids before your dad realizes what's happened and dies, his hopes reduced to a few chat-tering teeth and a pack of pornographic playing cards. Yeah—great things come to the U.S. out of Hong Kong.

STEVE. *(Lights a cigarette, blows smoke, stands.)* Such as your parents? *(Steve turns on the music, exits. Blackout.)*

Scene 2

Lights up on Dale and Steve eating. It is a few minutes later and food is on the table. Dale eats Chinese style, vigorously shoveling food into his mouth. Steve picks. Grace enters carry-ing a jar of hot sauce. Steve sees her.

STEVE. *(To Grace.)* After eating, you like to go dance?

DALE. *(Face in bowl.)* No, thanks. I think we'd be con-spicuous.

STEVE. *(To Grace.)* Like to go dance?

GRACE. Perhaps. We will see.

DALE. *(To Steve.)* Wait a minute. Hold on. How can you just...? I'm here, too, you know. Don't forget I exist just 'cuz you can't understand me.

STEVE. Please repeat?

DALE. I get better communication from my fish. Look, we go see movie. Three here. See? One, two, three. Three can see movie. Only two can dance.

STEVE. *(To Grace.)* I ask you to go dance.

30

GRACE. True, but...

DALE. *(To Grace.)* That would really be a screw, you know? You invite me down here, you don't have anyone for me to go out with, but you decide to go dancing.

GRACE. Dale, I understand.

DALE. Understand? That would really be a screw. *(To Steve.)* Look, if you wanna dance, go find yourself some nice FOB partner.

STEVE. "FOB"? Has what meaning?

GRACE. Dale...

DALE. F-O-B. Fresh Off the Boat. FOB.

GRACE. Dale, I agree.

DALE. See, we both agree. *(To Grace.)* He's a pretty prime example, isn't he? All those foreign students—

GRACE. I mean, I agree about going dancing.

DALE. —go swimming in their underwear and everything— What?

GRACE. *(To Steve.)* Please understand. This is not the right time for dancing.

STEVE. Okay.

DALE. "Okay." It's okay when *she* says it's okay.

STEVE. *(To Dale.)* "Fresh Off Boat" has what meaning? *(Pause.)*

DALE. *(To Grace.)* Did you ever hear about Dad his first year in the U.S.?

GRACE. Dale, he wants to know...

DALE. Well, Gung Gung was pretty rich back then, so Dad must've been a pretty disgusting...one, too. You know, his first year here, he spent like, thirteen thousand dollars. And that was back 'round 1950.

GRACE. Well, Mom never got anything.

STEVE. FOB means what?

DALE. That's probably 'cause women didn't get anything back then. Anyway, he bought himself a new car—all kinds of stuff, I guess. But then Gung Gung went bankrupt, so Dad had to work.

31

GRACE. And Mom starved.

DALE. Couldn't hold down a job. Wasn't used to taking orders from anyone.

GRACE. Mom was used to taking orders from everyone.

STEVE. Please explain this meaning.

DALE. Got fired from job after job. Something like fifteen in a year. He'd just walk in the front door and out the back, practically.

GRACE. Well, at least he had a choice of doors. At least he was educated.

STEVE. *(To Dale.)* Excuse!

DALE. Huh?

GRACE. He was educated. Here. In America. When Mom came over, she couldn't quit just 'cause she was mad at her employer. It was work or starve.

DALE. Well, Dad had some pretty lousy jobs, too.

STEVE. *(To Dale.)* Explain, please!

GRACE. Do you know what it's like to work eighty hours a week just to feed yourself?

DALE. Do you?

STEVE. Dale!

DALE. *(To Steve.)* It means you. You know how, if you go to a fish store or something, they have the stuff that just came in that day? Well, so have you.

STEVE. I do not understand.

DALE. Forget it. That's part of what makes you one. *(Pause.)*

STEVE. *(Picking up hot sauce, to Dale.)* Hot. You want some? *(Pause.)*

DALE. Well, yeah. Okay. Sure. *(Steve puts hot sauce on Dale's food.)* Hey, isn't that kinda a lot?

GRACE. See, Steve's family comes from Shanghai.

DALE. Hmmmmm. Well, I'll try it. *(He takes a gulp, puts down his food.)*

GRACE. I think perhaps that was too much for him.

DALE. No.

GRACE. Want some water?

32

DALE. Yes. *(Grace exits.)* You like hot sauce? You like your food hot? All right—here. *(He dumps the contents of the jar on Steve's plate, stirs.)* Fucking savage. Don't you ever worry about your intestines falling out? *(Grace enters, gives water to Dale. Steve sits shocked.)* Thanks. FOBs can eat anything, huh? They're specially trained. Helps maintain the characteristic greasy look. *(Steve, cautiously, begins to eat his food.)* What—? Look, Grace, he's eating that! He's amazing! A freak! What a cannibal!

GRACE. *(Taking Dale's plate.)* Want me to throw yours out?

DALE. *(Snatching it back.)* Huh? No. No, I can eat it. *(Dale and Steve stare at each other across the table. In unison, they pick up as large a glob of food as possible, stuff it into their mouths. They cough and choke. They rest, repeat the face-off a second time. They continue in silent pain. Grace, who has been watching this, speaks to us.)*

GRACE. Yeah. It's tough trying to live in Chinatown. But it's tough trying to live in Torrance, too. It's true. I don't like being alone. you know, when Mom could finally bring me to the U.S., I was already ten. But I never studied my English very hard in Taiwan, so I got moved back to the second grade. There were a few Chinese girls in the fourth grade, but they were American-born, so they wouldn't even talk to me. They'd just stay with themselves and compare how much clothes they all had, and make fun of the way we all talked. I figured I had a better chance of getting in with the white kids than with them, so in junior high I started bleaching my hair and hanging out at the beach—you know, Chinese hair looks pretty lousy when you bleach it. After a while, I knew what beach was gonna be good on any given day, and I could tell who was coming just by his van. But the American-born Chinese, it didn't matter to them. They just giggled and went to their own dances. Until my senior year in high school—that's how long it took for me to get over this whole thing. One night I took Dad's car and drove on Hollywood Boulevard, all the way from downtown to Beverly Hills, then back on Sunset. I was looking and listening—all the time with the window down, just so I'd feel like I was part of the city. And that Friday, it was—I guess—I said, "I'm lonely. And I don't like it. I don't like being alone." And that was all. As soon as I

33

said it, I felt all of the breeze—it was really cool on my face—and I heard all of the radio—and the music sounded really good, you know? So I drove home. *(Pause. Dale bursts out coughing.)* Oh, I'm sorry. Want some more water, Dale?

DALE. It's okay. I'll get it myself. *(He exits.)*

STEVE. *(Looks at Grace.)* Good, huh? *(Steve and Grace stare at each other, as lights fade to black.)*

ACT II

In blackout.

DALE. I am much better now. *(Single spot on Dale.)* I go out now. Lots. I can, anyway. Sometimes I don't ask anyone, so I don't go out. But I could. *(Pause.)* I am much better now. I have friends now. Lots. They drive Porsche Carreras. Well, one does. He has a house up in the Hollywood Hills where I can stand and look down on the lights of L.A. I guess I haven't really been there yet. But I could easily go. I'd just have to ask. *(Pause.)* My parents—they don't know nothing about the world, about watching Benson at the Roxy, about ordering *hors d'oeuvres* at Scandia's, downshifting onto the Ventura Freeway at midnight. They're yellow ghosts and they've tried to cage me up with Chinese-ness when all the time we were in America. *(Pause.)* So, I've had to work real hard—real hard—to be myself. To not be a Chinese, a yellow, a slant, a gook. To be just a human being, like everyone else, *(Pause.)* I've paid my dues. And that's why I am much better now. I'm making it, you know? I'm making it in America. *(A napkin is thrown in front of Dale's face from R. As it passes, the lights go up. The napkin falls on what we recognize as the dinner table from the last scene. We are in the back room. Dinner is over. Steve has thrown the napkin from where he is sitting in his chair. Dale is standing U. of the table and had been talking to Steve.)* So, look, will you just not be so...Couldn't you just be a little more...? I mean, we don't have to do all this...You know what's gonna happen to us tomorrow morning? *(He burps.)* What kinda diarrhea...? Look, maybe if you could just be a little more... *(He gropes.)* normal. Here—stand up. *(Steve does.)* Don't smile like that. Okay. You ever see *Saturday Night Fever?*
STEVE. Oh. *Saturday...*
DALE. Yeah.
STEVE. Oh. *Saturday Night Fever.* Disco.

DALE. That's it. Okay. You know...

STEVE. John Travolta.

DALE. Right. John Travolta. Now, maybe if you could be a little more like him.

STEVE. Uh—Bee Gees?

DALE. Yeah, right. Bee Gees. But what I mean is...

STEVE. You like Bee Gees?

DALE. I dunno. They're okay. Just stand a little more like him, you know, his walk? *(Dale tries to demonstrate.)*

STEVE. I believe Bee Gees very good.

DALE. Yeah. Listen.

STEVE. You see movie name of...

DALE. Will you listen for a sec?

STEVE. ...*Grease?*

DALE. Hold on!

STEVE. Also Bee Gees.

DALE. I'm trying to help you!

STEVE. Also John Travolta?

DALE. I'm trying to get you normal!

STEVE. And—Oliver John-Newton.

DALE. WILL YOU SHUT UP? I'M TRYING TO HELP YOU! I'M TRYING...

STEVE. Very good!

DALE. ...TO MAKE YOU LIKE JOHN TRAVOLTA! *(Dale grabs Steve by the arm. Pause. Steve coldly knocks Dale's hands away. Dale picks up the last of the dirty dishes on the table and backs into the kitchen. Grace enters from the kitchen with the box wrapped in Act I. She sits in a chair and goes over the wrapping, her back to Steve. He gets up and begins to go for the box, almost reaching her. She turns around suddenly, though, at which point he drops to the floor and pretends to be looking for something. She then turns back front, and he resumes his attempt. Just as he reaches the kitchen door, Dale enters with a wet sponge. To Steve.)* Oh, you finally willing to help? I already brought in all the dishes, you know. Here—wipe the table. *(Dale gives sponge to Steve, returns to kitchen. Steve throws the sponge on the floor, sits back at table. Grace turns around, sees sponge on the floor, picks it up, and goes to wipe the table. She brings the box with her and holds it in one hand.)*

GRACE. Look—you've been wanting this for some time now. Okay. Here. I'll give it to you. *(She puts it on the table.)* A welcome to this country. You don't have to fight for it—I'll give it to you instead. *(Pause; Steve pushes the box off the table.)* Okay. Your choice. *(Grace wipes the table.)*

DALE. *(Entering from kitchen; sees Grace.)* What—you doing this?

GRACE. Don't worry, Dale.

DALE. I asked him to do it.

GRACE. I'll do it.

DALE. I asked him to do it. He's useless! *(Dale takes the sponge.)* Look, I don't know how much English you know, but look-ee! *(He uses a mock Chinese accent.)*

GRACE. Dale, don't do that.

DALE. *(Using sponge.)* Look—makes table all clean, see?

GRACE. You have to understand...

DALE. Ooooh! Nice and clean!

GRACE. ...he's not used to this.

DALE. "Look! I can see myself!"

GRACE. Look, I can do this. Really.

DALE. Here—now you do. *(Dale forces Steve's hand onto the sponge.)* Good. Very good. Now, move it around. *(Dale leads Steve's hand.)* Oh, you learn so fast. Get green card, no time flat, buddy. *(Dale removes his hand; Steve stops.)* Uh-uh-uh. You must do it yourself. Come. There—now doesn't that make you feel proud? *(He takes his hand off; Steve stops. Dales gives up, crosses D. Steve remains at the table, still.)* Jesus! I'd trade him in for a vacuum cleaner any day.

GRACE. You shouldn't humiliate him like that.

DALE. What humiliate? I asked him to wipe the table, that's all.

GRACE. See, he's different. He probably has a lot of servants at home.

DALE. Big deal. He's in America, now. He'd better learn to work.

GRACE. He's rich, you know.

DALE. So what? They all are. Rich FOBs.

GRACE. Does that include me?

DALE. Huh?

GRACE. Does that include me? Am I one of your "rich FOBs"?

DALE. What? Grace, c'mon, that's ridiculous. You're not rich. I mean, you're not poor, but you're not rich either. I mean, you're not a FOB. FOBs are different. You've been over here most of your life. You've had time to thaw out. You've thawed out really well, and besides—you're my cousin. *(Dale strokes Grace's hair, and they freeze as before. Steve, meanwhile, has almost imperceptibly begun to clean with his sponge. He speaks to the audience as if speaking with his family.)*

STEVE. Yes. I will go to America. "Mei Guo." *(Pause. He begins working.)* The white ghosts came into the harbor today. They promised that they would bring us to America, and that in America we would never want for anything. One white ghost told how the streets are paved with diamonds, how the land is so rich that pieces of gold lie on the road, and the worker-devils consider them too insignificant even to bend down for. They told of a land where there are no storms, no snow, but sunshine and warmth all year round, where a man could live out in the open and feel not even discomfort from the nature around him—a worker's paradise. A land of gold, a mountain of wealth, a land in which a man can make his fortune and grow without wrinkles into an old age. And the white ghosts are providing free passage both ways. *(Pause.)* All we need to do is sign a worker's contract. *(Pause.)* Yes, I am going to America. *(At this point, Grace and Dale become mobile, but still fail to hear Steve. Grace picks up the box.)*

DALE. What's that?

STEVE. *(His wiping becomes increasingly frenzied.)* I am going to America because of its promises. I am going to follow the white ghosts because of their promises.

DALE. Is this for me?

STEVE. Because they promised! They promised! AND LOOK!

38

YOU PROMISED! THIS IS SHIT! IT'S NOT TRUE.

DALE. *(Taking the box.)* Let's see what's inside, is that okay?

STEVE. *(Shoves Dale to the ground and takes the box.)* IT IS NOT! *(With accent.)* THIS IS MINE!

DALE. Well, what kind of shit is that?

STEVE. She gave this to me.

DALE. What kind of...we're not at your place. We're not in Hong Kong, you know. Look—look all around you—you see shit on the sidewalks?

STEVE. This is mine!

DALE. You see armies of rice-bowl haircuts?

STEVE. She gave this to me!

DALE. People here have their flies zipped up—see?

STEVE. You should not look in it.

DALE. So we're not in Hong Kong. And I'm not one of your servant boys that you can knock around—that you got by trading in a pack of pornographic playing cards—that you probably deal out to your friends. You're in America, understand?

STEVE. Quiet! Do you know who I am?

DALE. Yeah—you're a FOB. You're a rich FOB in the U.S. But you better watch yourself. 'Cause you can be sent back.

STEVE. Shut up! Do you know who I am?

DALE. You can be sent back, you know—just like that. 'Cause you're a guest here, understand?

STEVE. *(To Grace.)* Tell him who I am.

DALE. I know who he is—heir to a fortune in junk merchandise. Big deal. Like being heir to Captain Crunch.

STEVE. Tell him! *(Silence.)*

GRACE. You know it's not like that.

STEVE. Tell him!

DALE. Huh?

GRACE. All the stuff about rice bowls and—zippers—have you ever been there, Dale?

DALE. Well, yeah. Once. When I was ten.

GRACE. Well, it's changed a lot.

DALE. Remember getting heat rashes.

39

GRACE. People are dressing really well now—and the whole place has become really stylish—well, certainly not everybody, but the people who are well-off enough to send their kids to American colleges—they're really kinda classy.

DALE. Yeah.

GRACE. Sort of.

DALE. You mean, like him. So what? It's easy to be classy when you're rich.

GRACE. All I'm saying is...

DALE. Hell, I could do that.

GRACE. Huh?

DALE. I could be classy, too, if I was rich.

GRACE. You *are* rich.

DALE. No. Just upper-middle. Maybe.

GRACE. Compared to us, you're rich.

DALE. No, not really. And especially not compared to him. Besides, when I was born we were still poor.

GRACE. Well, you're rich now.

DALE. Used to get one Life Saver a day.

GRACE. That's all? One Life Saver?

DALE. Well, I mean, that's not all I lived on. We got normal food, too.

GRACE. I know, but...

DALE. Not like we were living in cardboard boxes or anything.

GRACE. All I'm saying is that the people who are coming in now—a lot of them are different—they're already real Westernized. They don't act like they're fresh off the boat.

DALE. Maybe. But they're still FOBs.

STEVE. Tell him who I am!

DALE. Anyway, real nice dinner, Grace. I really enjoyed it.

GRACE. Thank you.

STEVE. Okay! I will tell myself.

DALE. Go tell yourself—just don't bother us.

GRACE. *(Standing, to Steve.)* What would you like to do now?

STEVE. Huh?

GRACE. You wanted to go out after dinner?

STEVE. Yes, yes. We go out.

DALE. I'll drive. You sent the hearse home.

STEVE. I tell driver—return car after dinner.

DALE. How could you...? What time did you...? When did you tell him to return? What time?

STEVE. *(Looks at his watch.)* Seven-five.

DALE. No—not what time is it. What time you tell him to return?

STEVE. Seven-five. Go see. *(Dale exits through kitchen. No accent.)* Why wouldn't you tell him who I am?

GRACE. Can Gwan Gung die? *(Pause.)*

STEVE. No warrior can defeat Gwan Gung.

GRACE. Does Gwan Gung fear ghosts?

STEVE. Gwan Gung fears no ghosts.

GRACE. Ghosts of warriors?

STEVE. No warrior ghosts.

GRACE. Ghosts that avenge?

STEVE. No avenging ghosts.

GRACE. Ghosts forced into exile?

STEVE. No exiled ghosts.

GRACE. Ghosts that wait? *(Pause.)*

STEVE. *(Quietly.)* May I...take you out tonight? Maybe not tonight, but some other time? Another time? *(He strokes her hair.)* What has happened?

DALE. *(Entering.)* I cannot believe it... *(He sees them.)* What do you think you're doing? *(He grabs Steve's hand. To Steve.)* What...I step out for one second and you just go an—hell, you FOBs are sneaky. No wonder they check you so close at Immigration.

GRACE. Dale, I can really take care of myself.

DALE. Yeah? What was his hand doing, then?

GRACE. Stroking my hair.

DALE. Well, yeah. I could see that. I mean, what was it doing stroking your hair? *(Pause.)* Uh, never mind. All I'm saying is... *(He gropes.)* Jesus! If you want to be alone, why don't you just say so, huh? If that's what you really want, just say it, okay? *(Pause.)* Okay. Time's up.

GRACE. Was the car out there?

DALE. Huh? Yeah. Yeah, it was. I could not believe it. I go out-side and—thank God—there's no limousine. Just as I'm about to come back, I hear this sound like the roar of death and this big black shadow scraped up beside me. I could not believe it!

STEVE. Car return—seven-five.

DALE. And when I asked him—I asked the driver, what time he'd been told to return. And he just looks at me and says, "Now."

STEVE. We go out?

DALE. What's going on here? What is this?

STEVE. Time to go.

DALE. No! Not till you explain what's going on.

STEVE. *(To Grace.)* You now want to dance?

DALE. *(To Grace.)* Do you understand this? Was this coincidence?

STEVE. *(Ditto.)* I am told good things of American discos.

DALE. *(Ditto.)* You and him just wanna go off by yourselves?

STEVE. I hear of Dillon's.

DALE. Is that it?

STEVE. You hear of Dillon's?

DALE. It's okay, you know.

STEVE. In Westwood.

DALE. I don't mind.

STEVE. Three—four stories.

DALE. Really.

STEVE. Live band.

DALE. Cousin.

STEVE. We go. *(He takes Grace's hand.)*

DALE. He's just out to snake you, you know. *(He takes the other hand. From this point on, almost unnoticeable, the lights begin to dim.)*

GRACE. Okay! That's enough! *(She pulls away.)* That's enough! I have to make all the decisions around here, don't I? When I leave it up to you two, the only place we go is in circles.

DALE. Well...

STEVE. No, I am suggesting place to go.

GRACE. Look, Dale, when I asked you here, what did I say we were going to do?

DALE. Uh—dinner and a movie—or something. But it was a different "we," then.

GRACE. It doesn't matter. That's what we're going to do.

DALE. I'll drive.

STEVE. My car can take us to movie.

GRACE. I think we better not drive at all. We'll stay right here. *(She removes Steve's tie.)* Do you remember this?

DALE. What—you think I borrow clothes or something? Hell, I don't even wear ties. *(Grace takes the tie, wraps it around Dale's face like a blindfold.)* Grace, what are you...?

GRACE. *(To Steve.)* Do you remember this?

DALE. I already told you. I don't need a closer look or nothing.

STEVE. Yes.

GRACE. *(Ties the blindfold, releases it.)* Let's sit down.

DALE. Wait.

STEVE. You want me to sit here?

DALE. Grace, is he understanding you?

GRACE. Have you ever played Group Story?

STEVE. Yes, I have played that.

DALE. There—there he goes again! Grace, I'm gonna take... *(He starts to remove the blindfold.)*

GRACE. *(Stopping him.)* Dale, listen or you won't understand.

DALE. But how come *he's* understanding?

GRACE. Because he's listening.

DALE. But...

GRACE. Now, let's play Group Story.

DALE. Not again. Grace, that's only good when you're stoned.

GRACE. Who wants to start? Steve, you know the rules?

STEVE. Yes—I understand.

DALE. See, we're talking normal speed—and he still understood.

GRACE. Dale, would you like to start? *(Pause.)*

DALE. All right. *(By this time, the lights have dimmed, throwing shadows on the stage. Grace will strike two pots together to indicate each speaker change and the ritual will gradually take on elements of Chinese opera.)* Uh, once upon a time...there were...three bears—Grace, this is ridiculous!

GRACE. Tell a story.

DALE. ...three bears and they each had...cancer of the lymph nodes. Uh—and they were very sad. So the baby bear said, "I'll go to the new Cedar Sinai Hospital, where they may have a cure for this fatal illness."

GRACE. But the new Cedar Sinai Hospital happened to be two thousand miles away—across the ocean.

STEVE. *(Gradually losing his accent.)* That is very far.

DALE. How did—? So, the bear tried to swim over, but his leg got chewed off by alligators—are there alligators in the Pacific Ocean?—Oh, well. So he ended up having to go for a leg *and* a cure for malignant cancer of the lymph nodes.

GRACE. When he arrived there, he came face to face with—

STEVE. With Gwan Gung, god of warriors, writers, and prostitutes.

DALE. And Gwan Gung looked at the bear and said...

GRACE. ...strongly and with spirit...

STEVE. "One-legged bear, what are you doing on my land? You are from America, are you not?"

DALE. And the bear said, "Yes. Yes."

GRACE. And Gwan Gung replied...

STEVE. *(Getting up.)* By stepping forward, sword drawn, ready to wound, not kill, not end it so soon. To draw it out, play it, taunt it, make it feel like a dog.

DALE. Which is probably rather closely related to the bear.

GRACE. Gwan Gung said—

STEVE. "When I came to America, did you lick my wounds? When I came to America, did you cure my sickness?"

DALE. And just as Gwan Gung was about to strike—

GRACE. There arrived Fa Mu Lan, the Woman Warrior. *(She stands, faces Steve. From here on in, striking pots together is not needed.)* "Gwan Gung."

44

STEVE. "What do you want? Don't interfere! Don't forget, I have gone before you into battle many times."

DALE. But Fa Mu Lan seemed not to hear Gwan Gung's warning. She stood between him and the bear, drawing out her own sword.

GRACE. "You will learn I cannot forget. I don't forget, Gwan Gung. Spare the bear and I will present gifts."

STEVE. "Very well. He is hardly worth killing."

DALE. And the bear hopped off. Fa Mu Lan pulled a parcel from beneath her gown. *(She removes Dale's blindfold.)* She pulled out two items.

GRACE. "This is for you." *(She hands blindfold to Steve.)*

STEVE. "What is that?"

DALE. She showed him a beautiful piece of red silk, thick enough to be opaque, yet so light, he barely felt it in his hands.

GRACE. "Do you remember this?"

STEVE. "Why, yes. I used this silk for sport one day. How did you get hold of it?"

DALE. Then she presented him with a second item. It was a fabric—thick and dried and brittle.

GRACE. "Do you remember this?"

STEVE. *(Turning away.)* "No, no. I've never seen this before in my life. This has nothing to do with me. What is it—a dragon skin?"

DALE. Fa Mu Lan handed it to Gwan Gung.

GRACE. "Never mind. Use it—as a tablecloth. As a favor to me."

STEVE. "It's much too hard and brittle. But, to show you my graciousness in receiving—I will use it tonight!"

DALE. That night, Gwan Gung had a large banquet, at which there was plenty, even for the slaves. But Fa Mu Lan ate nothing. She waited until midnight, till Gwan Gung and the gods were full of wine and empty of sense. Sneaking behind him, she pulled out the tablecloth, waving it about her head.

GRACE. *(Ripping the tablecloth from the table.)* "Gwan Gung, you foolish boy. This thing you have used tonight as a tablecloth—it is the stretched and dried skins of my fathers. My fathers, whom you slew—for sport! and you have been eating their sins—you ate them!"

STEVE. "No. I was blindfolded. I did not know."

DALE. Fa Mu Lan waved the skin before Gwan Gung's face. It smelled suddenly of death.

GRACE. "Remember the day you played? Remember? Well, eat that day, Gwan Gung."

STEVE. "I am not responsible. No. No." *(Grace throws one end of the tablecloth to Dale, who catches it. Together, they become like Steve's parents. They chase him about the stage, waving the tablecloth like a net.)*

DALE. Yes!

GRACE. Yes!

STEVE. No!

DALE. You must!

GRACE. Go!

STEVE. Where?

DALE. To America!

GRACE. To work!

STEVE. Why?

DALE. Because!

GRACE. We need!

STEVE. No!

DALE. Why?

GRACE. Go.

STEVE. Hard!

DALE. So?

GRACE. Need.

STEVE. Far!

DALE. So?

GRACE. Need!

STEVE. Safe!

DALE. Here?

GRACE. No!

STEVE. Why?

DALE. Them. *(Points.)*
GRACE. Them. *(Points.)*
STEVE. Won't!
DALE. Must!
GRACE. Must!
STEVE. Won't!
DALE. Go!
GRACE. Go!
STEVE. Won't!
DALE. Bye!
GRACE. Bye!
STEVE. Won't!
DALE. Fare!
GRACE. Well! *(Dale and Grace drop the tablecloth over Steve, who sinks to the floor. Grace then moves offstage, into the bathroom—storage room, while Dale goes U. and stands with his back to the audience. Silence.)*
STEVE. *(Begins pounding the ground.)* Nooooo! *(He throws off the tablecloth, standing up full. Lights up full, blindingly.)* I am GWAN GUNG!
DALE. *(Turning D. suddenly.)* What...?
STEVE. I HAVE COME TO THIS LAND TO STUDY!
DALE. Grace...
STEVE. TO STUDY THE ARTS OF WAR, OF LITERA-TURE, OF RIGHTEOUSNESS!
DALE. A movie's fine.
STEVE. I FOUGHT THE WARS OF THE THREE KINGDOMS!
DALE. An ordinary movie, let's go.
STEVE. I FOUGHT WITH THE FIRST PIONEERS, THE FIRST WARRIORS THAT CHOSE TO FOLLOW THE WHITE GHOSTS TO THIS LAND!
DALE. You can pick okay?
STEVE. I WAS THEIR HERO, THEIR LEADER, THEIR FIRE!
DALE. I'll even let him drive, how's that?

47

STEVE. AND THIS LAND IS MINE! IT HAS NO RIGHT TO TREAT ME THIS WAY!

GRACE. No. Gwan Gung, *you* have no rights.

STEVE. Who's speaking?

GRACE. *(Enters with a* da dao *and* mao, *two swords.)* It is Fa Mu Lan. You are in a new land, Gwan Gung.

STEVE. Not new—I have been here before, many times. This time, I said I will have it easy. I will come as no ChinaMan before— on a plane, with money and rank.

GRACE. And?

STEVE. And—there is no change. I am still treated like this! This land...has no right. I AM GWAN GUNG!

GRACE. And I am Fa Mu Lan.

DALE. I'll be Chiang Kai-shek, how's that?

STEVE. *(To Dale.)* You! How can you—? I came over with your parents.

GRACE. *(Turning to Steve.)* We are in America. And we have a battle to fight. *(She tosses the* da dao *to Steve. They square off.)*

STEVE. I don't want to fight you.

GRACE. You killed my family.

STEVE. You were revenged—I ate your father's sins.

GRACE. That's not revenge! *(Swords strike.)* That was only the tease. *(Strike.)* What's the point in dying if you don't know the cause of your death? *(Series of strikes. Steve falls.)*

DALE. Okay! that's it! *(Grace stands over Steve, her sword pointed at his heart. Dale snatches the sword from her hands. She does not move.)* Jesus! Enough is enough! *(Dale takes Steve's sword; he also does not react.)* What the hell kind of movie was that? *(Dale turns his back on the couple, heads for the bathroom—storageroom. Grace uses her now invisible sword to thrust in and out of Steve's heart once.)* That's it. Game's over. Now just sit down here. Breathe. One. Two. One. Two. Air. Good stuff. Glad they made it. Right, cousin? *(Dale strokes Grace's hair. They freeze. Steve rises slowly to his knees and delivers a monologue to the audience.)*

STEVE. Ssssh! Please, miss! Please—quiet! I will not hurt you, I promise. All I want is...food...anything. You look full of plenty. I have not eaten almost one week now, but four days past when I found one egg and I ate every piece of it—including shell. Every piece, I ate. Please. Don't you have anything extra? *(Pause.)* I want to. Now. This land does not want us any more than China. But I cannot. All work was done, then the bosses said they could not send us back. And I am running, running from Eureka, running from San Francisco, running from Los Angeles. And I been eating very little. One egg, only. *(Pause.)* All America wants ChinaMen go home, but no one want it bad enough to pay our way. Now, please, can't you give even little? *(Pause.)* I ask you, what you hate most? What work most awful for white woman? *(Pause.)* Good. I will do that thing for you—you can give me food. *(Pause.)* Think—you relax, you are given those things, clean, dry, press. No scrub, no dry. It is wonderful thing I offer you. *(Pause.)* Good. Give me those and please bring food, or I be done before these things. *(Grace steps away from Dale with box.)*

GRACE. Here—I've brought you something. *(She hands him the box.)* Open it. *(He hesitates, then does, and takes out a small* chong you bing.) Eat it. *(He does, slowly at first, then ravenously.)* Good. Eat it all down. It's just food. Really. Feel better now? Good. Eat the *bing.* Hold it in your hands. Your hands...are beautiful. Lift it to your mouth. Your mouth...is beautiful. Bite it with your teeth. Your teeth...are beautiful. Crush it with your tongue. Your tongue...is beautiful. Slide it down your throat. Your throat...is beautiful.

STEVE. Our hands are beautiful. *(She holds hers next to his.)*

GRACE. What do you see?

STEVE. I see...I see the hands of warriors.

GRACE. Warriors? What of gods then?

STEVE. There are no gods that travel. Only warriors travel. *(Silence.)* Would you like go dance?

GRACE. Yeah. Sure. Okay. *(They start to leave. Dale speaks softly.)*

DALE. Well, if you want to be alone...

GRACE. I think we would, Dale. Is that okay? *(Pause.)* Thanks for coming over. I'm sorry things got so screwed up.

DALE. Oh—uh—that's okay. The evening was real...different, anyway.

GRACE. Yeah. Maybe you can take Frank off the tracks now?
DALE. *(Laughing softly.)* Yeah. Maybe I will.
STEVE. *(To Dale.)* Very nice meeting you. *(Extends his hand.)*
DALE. *(Does not take it.)* Yeah. Same here. *(Steve and Grace start to leave.)* You know...I think you picked up English faster than anyone I've ever met. *(Pause.)*
STEVE. Thank you.
GRACE. See you.
STEVE. Good-bye.
DALE. Bye. *(Grace and Steve exit.)*

CODA

Dale alone in the back room. He examines the swords, the tablecloth, the box. He sits down.

DALE. F-O-B. Fresh Off the Boat. FOB. Clumsy, ugly, greasy FOB. Loud, stupid, four-eyed FOB. Big feet. Horny. Like Lenny in *Of Mice and Men.* F-O-B. Fresh Off the Boat. FOB

SLOW FADE TO BLACK

PROPERTY LIST

PROLOGUE
Blackboard

ACT ONE — SCENE 1
Table, with tablecloth
Chairs
Small radio
Partially wrapped box, with wrapped gift box inside
Scotch tape
Telephone
Menu
Cigarettes (Steve)

ACT ONE — SCENE 2
Bowls of Chinese food
Jar of hot sauce
Glass of water

ACT TWO
Napkins
Wet sponge
Wrapped box
Watch (Steve)
Swords (2)
Box, with Chinese pancake

THE HOUSE OF
SLEEPING BEAUTIES

From the Short Story
by Yasunari Kawabata

For Natolie

This play is a fantasy. In historical fact, Kawabata's composition of his novelette, *House of the Sleeping Beauties,* and his unexplained suicide occurred many years apart.

Many people helped me develop this play, and I'd like to thank especially Grafton Mouen, Jean Brody, John Harnagel, Marcy Mattox, Natolie Miyawaki, Nancy Takahashi, Mitch Motooka, and Helen Merrill.

CHARACTERS

YASUNARI KAWABATA, *72, a leading Japanese novelist.*

WOMAN, *Japanese, late seventies.*

SYNOPSIS OF SCENES

Scene 1. The sitting room of the House of Sleeping Beauties. Night.

Scene 2. The sitting room, following evening.

Scene 3. The sitting room, several months later, evening.

Scene 4. The sitting room, one week later, evening.

TIME

1972

PLACE

Tokyo

THE HOUSE
OF SLEEPING BEAUTIES

Scene 1

A sitting room. Not richly decorated. Desk, pillows, low table, equipment for tea, cabinet, screen, mirror, furnace. Night. Woman sits at desk, writing. Kawabata paces.

WOMAN. Now, you mustn't do anything distasteful.

KAWABATA. Distasteful?

WOMAN. You mustn't stick your fingers in the girl's mouth, or anything like that.

KAWABATA. Oh, no. I wouldn't think of it.

WOMAN. Good. All my guests are gentlemen.

KAWABATA. Would you please put that down?

WOMAN. *(Indicating the pen.)* This?

KAWABATA. Yes. I'm not here to be interviewed.

WOMAN. Perhaps. *I* am, however, accountable to my girls—

KAWABATA. Fine.

WOMAN. —and must therefore ask a few questions of those who wish to become my guests.

KAWABATA. You assume too easily, madame.

WOMAN. Oh?

KAWABATA. You asume that my presence here identifies me as just one type of man.

WOMAN. On the contrary, sir.

KAWABATA. Why did you assume I was going in there, then?

WOMAN. I never assumed any such thing. Did you assume I was going to allow you in there? *(Pause.)*

KAWABATA. "Allow me"?

WOMAN. Actually, I identify two types of men, sir—gentlemen and those who do not behave. My guests are all gentlemen. They do not disgrace the house. Obviously, very few men meet these requirements.

KAWABATA. What are you talking about?

WOMAN. I must protect my girls, and the house.

KAWABATA. Well, I mean, I'm certainly not going to assault a girl, if that's what you mean. Is that what you think? That I look like a man who goes to brothels?

WOMAN. Neither looks nor brothels has much to do with it, sir. My experience has taught me that in most cases, scratch a man and you'll find a molester.

KAWABATA. Well, if you take that kind of attitude...

WOMAN. A look in most men's bottom drawers confirms this.

KAWABATA. ...how is any man to prove he's a...a gentleman, as you say?

WOMAN. I take a risk on all my guests. But I have my methods; I judge as best I can.

KAWABATA. That's ridiculous. That men must be...tested to become your customers. But all your customers are practically ghosts anyway—of course they don't object. Their throats are too dry to protest.

WOMAN. Guests.

KAWABATA. I'm sorry?

WOMAN. They're not customers, they're guests.

KAWABATA. Well, I, for one, do not intend to become a guest, understand?

WOMAN. You are very proud.

KAWABATA. Proud?

WOMAN. But that doesn't necessarily mean you are not a gentleman. Sometimes the proudest men are the best behaved. So, you don't want to be my guest. What *do* you want?

KAWABATA. I only want to talk.

WOMAN. About what?

KAWABATA. Your house.

WOMAN. Shopping?

KAWABATA. No.

WOMAN. I'm sorry.

KAWABATA. I want to know why the old men come here.

WOMAN. But all your answers are in there.

KAWABATA. No, they're not. I could never feel what they feel, what brings them back—a parade of corpses—night after night. But you—perhaps they share their secrets.

WOMAN. I have no secrets.

KAWABATA. Old Eguchi—

WOMAN. And I'm no gossip.

KAWABATA. He talked to me last week.

WOMAN. Yes, he called and said you were coming.

KAWABATA. Said he comes here almost every night. I wanted him to tell me more, but he said I could only know more by talking to you.

WOMAN. He said you wished to gain entrance.

KAWABATA. No—he's making the same mistake as you. I won't be able to feel what he feels because my mind's different.

WOMAN. Oh?

KAWABATA. Eguchi's so old.

WOMAN. And you're young?

KAWABATA. Well, no. Not in years.

WOMAN. Oh.

KAWABATA. But my mind is young. Eguchi's is gone. He sits on his *futon* each afternoon swatting bees with tissue paper. Listen, I know you're a woman of business—may I offer you some fee for what you know?

WOMAN. Money?

KAWABATA. Don't worry. I'm not with the police or anything.

WOMAN. Don't be ridiculous. What do you take me for?

KAWABATA. What do I—?

WOMAN. You might as well pay me to tell you how one falls in love.

KAWABATA. What do you take yourself for, madame—acting like a sorceress, a *sensei*. You're just an old woman running this house. I have questions, and I'm willing to pay for the answers.

WOMAN. I have questions also. Fair, sir? *(Pause.)* How old are you?

KAWABATA. I won't answer just anything, you know.

WOMAN. Don't worry. Neither will I.

KAWABATA. Seventy-two.

WOMAN. Married?

KAWABATA. My wife passed away...several years ago.

WOMAN. I'm sorry. Children?

KAWABATA. Yes. Two. Daughters. Why are you asking this?

WOMAN. Don't worry. I'm no gossip. Retired?

KAWABATA. Uh—no...I mean, yes.

WOMAN. Yes or no?

KAWABATA. Uh—no.

WOMAN. No? No. Profession?

KAWABATA. Uh—teacher.

WOMAN. Teacher.

KAWABATA. University level, of course.

WOMAN. There. That wasn't so bad, was it?

KAWABATA. That's all?

WOMAN. Now, what would *you* like to know?

KAWABATA. From that, you decide?

WOMAN. I *would* like you to join me in a game, though.

KAWABATA. A game?

WOMAN. Yes. And as we play, we can talk about the rooms. Do you mind?

KAWABATA. Well, if it's harmless.

WOMAN. Quite. Would you like some tea?

KAWABATA. Oh, yes. Please. Thank you. This game— what's it called?

WOMAN. I don't know. It's old. Geishas used to play it with their customers, to relax them. *(She brings the tea, pours it.)*

KAWABATA. Relax? Perhaps it will relax me. *(He laughs softly.)* Now, why do you want me to play this? *(She pulls out of the desk a box, and opens it. Inside are twenty-five smooth tiles, five times as long as they are wide. While she speaks, she stacks them in five layers of five tiles each, such that the tiles of each layer are perpendicular to those of the layer below it.)*

WOMAN. So we can get to know each other. As I said, I must protect my girls from men who do not behave.

KAWABATA. You talk as if men should be put on leashes.

WOMAN. No, leashes aren't necessary at all. *(The tower is finished.)* There. We'll take turns removing tiles from the tower until it collapses. Understand?

KAWABATA. Is this a game you ask all your customers to play?

WOMAN. Guests. You can't touch the top layer, though, and you can only use one hand.

KAWABATA. But what's the object? Who wins, who loses?

WOMAN. There are no winners or losers. There is only the tower—intact or collapsed. Just one hand—like this. *(She removes a piece.)*

KAWABATA. My turn? What am I trying to do?

WOMAN. Judge the tiles. Wriggle that one, for instance—yes, that one you're touching—between your fingers. Is the weight of the stack on it? If so, don't force it. Leave it and look for another one that's looser. If you try to force the tiles to be what they're not, the whole thing will come crashing down.

KAWABATA. A test of skills? There *(He removes a piece.)* — your turn.

WOMAN. See? Simple.

KAWABATA. What kind of a test—? You're just an old woman. What kind of a contest is this?

WOMAN. Let's talk about you, sir. We want to make you happy. *(They continue to take turns through the following section.)*

KAWABATA. Happy? No, you don't understand. You can't—

WOMAN. Our guests sleep much better here. It's the warmth, they say.

KAWABATA. I don't have any trouble sleeping.

WOMAN. Don't you?

KAWABATA. Sometimes...sometimes I choose not to go to bed. But when I do, I sleep.

WOMAN. Our guests are never afraid to go to sleep.

KAWABATA. It's not that I'm afraid.

WOMAN. The darkness does not threaten them. *(Pause.)*
KAWABATA. Old Eguchi—he says that the girls...that they are naked.
WOMAN. Yes.
KAWABATA. He says they are very beautiful, but I hardly...
WOMAN. For you, I would pick an especially pretty one.
KAWABATA. For me—? Don't start—
WOMAN. How old was your wife when you first met her?
KAWABATA. My wife? Oh, I don't know. She must have been—oh, maybe nineteen.
WOMAN. Nineteen. That is a beautiful age. I would pick one who is nineteen.
KAWABATA. Don't be ridiculous. She'd see me and—
WOMAN. But you forget, sir—our girls won't see anything.
KAWABATA. I suppose you have some way of guaranteeing this. I suppose it's never happened that some girl has opened her eyes—
WOMAN. No. Never. *(Kawabata is having a particularly difficult time with a tile.)*
KAWABATA. Look at this. *(He holds out his hand, laughs.)* Shaking. Would you mind putting some more wood in the furnace?
WOMAN. Of course. *(She does so as she talks.)* I know what girl I would pick for you. She is half Japanese, half Caucasian. She has the most delicate hair—brown in one light, black in another. As she sleeps, she wriggles her left foot, like a cat, against the mattress, as if to draw out even the last bits of warmth. *(She returns to the table, sits. As she does, Kawabata causes the tower to fall.)*
KAWABATA. Ai! You shook it.
WOMAN. No. *(During the next session, she gets up, goes to the cabinet, removes a small jar filled with clear liquid and a tiny cup. She pours the liquid into the cup.)*
KAWABATA. Maybe an accident, but still—
WOMAN. I assure you.
KAWABATA. —when you sat down.
WOMAN. I was perfectly still.
KAWABATA. No, you shook the table.

WOMAN. I didn't touch it.

KAWABATA. Just a bit.

WOMAN. Really.

KAWABATA. But at the crucial moment.

WOMAN. Please, sir.

KAWABATA. Just as it was about to give.

WOMAN. Thank you for playing.

KAWABATA. It wasn't fair.

WOMAN. Please—

KAWABATA. It was my first time.

WOMAN. —take this cup.

KAWABATA. What?

WOMAN. Here. *(He takes it.)*

KAWABATA. What is this?

WOMAN. To help you sleep.

KAWABATA. Sleep?

WOMAN. To assure you a restful evening—in there. *(Pause.)* If you wish to, you may now go in. You're my guest. If you still have questions after tonight, I'll try to answer some—

KAWABATA. I can just—

WOMAN. —on your next visit.

KAWABATA. —go in?

WOMAN. Welcome. Your name?

KAWABATA. My name?

WOMAN. We keep names of all our guests.

KAWABATA. But I don't see why...

WOMAN. Our guests are our friends. Sometimes we like to let our friends know if we have something special. Don't worry. Confidential.

KAWABATA. Kawabata.

WOMAN. May I help you undress, Mr. Kawabata?

KAWABATA. Oh, yes. Thank you. *(They go behind the screen.)* I can just...go in?

WOMAN. Yes. On the right, second door. *(Pause.)* She's a very pretty girl.

KAWABATA. Second door.

WOMAN. On the right. She's asleep, waiting for you. *(Pause.)*
KAWABATA. I'm really only curious.
WOMAN. I know. That's why you should go in.
KAWABATA. What if...something happens?
WOMAN. Something?
KAWABATA. What if she wakes up?
WOMAN. Even if you were to try your utmost—you could cut off her arms and she wouldn't wake up till morning. Don't worry. *(They come out from behind the screen. He wears a light robe.)* Sleep well, Mr. Kawabata. A boy will wake you and bring you tea in the morning.
KAWABATA. Uh—thank you. *(She opens the door.)*
WOMAN. Listen.
KAWABATA. Listen?
WOMAN. To the waves. And the wind. *(Silence.)* Good night, Mr. Kawabata. *(He walks in. She closes the door. She moves to the table, begins cleaning up the tiles, as lights fade to black.)*

Scene 2

Following evening. Before the lights come up, we see a flame. Lights up. She sits at the desk. He is burning his record from yesterday, tosses it into the furnace.

KAWABATA. I'm not a teacher, madame. I'm a writer.
WOMAN. Oh. A writer?
KAWABATA. Have you read my novels, short stories?
WOMAN. Have you ever been published in this?
KAWABATA. *Shifuno Tomo?* Trash.
WOMAN. Then I haven't read you.
KAWABATA. I don't write about beauty tips *or* American movie stars.
WOMAN. So you're going to write a report on us.

63

KAWABATA. I'm not a reporter. I write stories, novels. For some time now, I've been thinking about old men. How it must—

WOMAN. If you wish to write your report, Mr. Kawabata, you must realize the consequences of your actions. You understand, don't you, that we can't let the outside know we're here. That would mean the end of the house.

KAWABATA. And that should worry me?

WOMAN. Does it? Didn't you sleep well?

KAWABATA. Hardly. I was afraid to touch the covers and disturb her. I studied the walls until I fell asleep, watched the colors change in the dark.

WOMAN. I see.

KAWABATA. But what I've learned about the state to which men come—to think they return—night after night—for that.

WOMAN. Then why have *you* returned?

KAWABATA. Me?

WOMAN. Why didn't you just write your report and destroy the house?

KAWABATA. Story. I wanted...to burn that.

WOMAN. Is that all?

KAWABATA. Yes. That's all. *(He chuckles.)* I certainly have no desire to repeat last night's experience. It's been so many years since I've had to share a bed. No room to stretch.

WOMAN. Well, then, go.

KAWABATA. What?

WOMAN. If you've done what you've come for, then you must want to leave.

KAWABATA. Yes. I will. But first, I thought I might talk...to you.

WOMAN. What about. You've burned your record, you're no longer a guest, you plan to write your report without concern for the house, my girls, or myself.

KAWABATA. Yourself?

WOMAN. Our relationship is hardly suited to polite conversation.

KAWABATA. You will be all right.

64

WOMAN. "All right." How can you be so insensitive? You talk like a man who lives in other men's beds.

KAWABATA. You are very defiant, madame. Defiance is admirable in a woman. Defiance in a man is nothing more than a trained response, since we always expect to get our way. But a woman's defiance is her own.

WOMAN. Mr. Kawabata, you must not write this report.

KAWABATA. What if I do?

WOMAN. Then my life is over.

KAWABATA. Don't be melodramatic.

WOMAN. Please. Don't talk of things you know nothing about. I can tell you. Only one other time—twenty years ago—have I ever misjudged a guest. He came back the next evening, as you have tonight, and informed me he was...with the authorities. Then he left. I didn't know what to do. First, I tried to imagine all the awful things that could happen, hoping that by picturing them, I would prevent them from taking place, since real life never happens like we envision it will. Finally, after an hour of this, I decided to sleep. As I lay in bed, I began to wonder, what else could I do? Where else could I go? I saw myself being carried up to Mount Obasute. My girls were carrying me up. "You're old now, Mama!" they cried. "We'll join your bones when we ourselves become old!" They left me in a cave and danced a *bon-odori* down the mountain, singing "Tokyo Ondo" as they went. *(She sings a little of it.)* I thought, "Look at them dancing. That's why I'm here and they're leaving me. Anyone who can dance down the mountain is free to go." And the next thing I knew, I was dancing a *bon-odori* right up there, on my bed—the springs making the sounds young people make in beds. And I danced down the hall to a telephone, and began looking for a new house for my girls. *(Pause.)* That was twenty years ago. Look at me today. I can't even raise a foot for three seconds, let alone dance. I'm old, and I have no savings, no money, no skills. This time, Mr. Kawabata, I would have to stay on Mount Obasute.

KAWABATA. Look, madame, even if I wrote this story, it's possible that your house wouldn't be affected.

WOMAN. Why? Don't people read them?

KAWABATA. Of course. But people will likely think it's all from my head. You haven't read my stories. Like what you said to me— "Listen to the waves," you said.

WOMAN. They often help men sleep.

KAWABATA. In one of my novels, the boy always makes love to the woman while listening to the waves. The critics would probably laugh, "Old Kawabata and waves. Can't he think of anything new?"

WOMAN. And if the authorities—some of whom already suspect our existence—if they read your story, that won't make them certain? *(Pause.)* What is that story to you?

KAWABATA. I want to write this story. I can do it. I know. I haven't written a story in...in...

WOMAN. That's just one story to you. This is my life.

KAWABATA. Better if you were rid of it.

WOMAN. Then you must change the facts—

KAWABATA. You made a mistake, madame.

WOMAN. —confuse the authorities.

KAWABATA. You chose not to cooperate with me yesterday.

WOMAN. But even that—

KAWABATA. You thought I was like the rest of them.

WOMAN. No, you mustn't write this report.

KAWABATA. You misjudged me. Now you see I'm different.

WOMAN. Yes, you are a reporter.

KAWABATA. You should have just told me about the house.

WOMAN. Mr. Kawabata—

KAWABATA. But you assumed—

WOMAN. —think of the girls.

KAWABATA. The girls?

WOMAN. The money they receive here.

KAWABATA. You shame them.

WOMAN. They are from poor families.

KAWABATA. They would be better off—

WOMAN. They come of their own will.

KAWABATA. —doing—working at...any other job.

WOMAN. And the old men.

KAWABATA. Don't tell me that.

WOMAN. We care about them. Look at this.

KAWABATA. At what?

WOMAN. At what you'll destroy.

KAWABATA. You humiliate them. Their despair—it's so great.

WOMAN. What do you know?

KAWABATA. Your girls—are they all still virgins?

WOMAN. Was yours?

KAWABATA. Yes. Do you see the depth of the old men's despair?

WOMAN. How do you know?

KAWABATA. That they can't even find the manhood to—

WOMAN. Mr. Kawabata, how do you know she was still a virgin? *(Pause.)*

KAWABATA. Don't worry. I didn't...molest her. I walked into the room. I didn't believe she was going to be naked. I knew you'd told me, but I thought, no, you couldn't go that far, it would be unfair to give men exactly what they want. But she was lying on her back, the blanket leaving bare two white shoulders and her neck. I couldn't see clearly yet, so I ran my fingers from one shoulder, across her neck, to the other shoulder. Nothing blocked my finger's path—nothing, no straps, only taut, smooth skin. I still couldn't believe it, so I placed my index finger at the base of her throat and moved down, under the blanket, further and further down—one unbroken line—all the way. When I knew, I pulled my hand away. She moaned and turned away from me. I looked at my finger, placed it at the top of her spine and followed the hard bumps all the way down. I looked at my finger again, tasted it. Then I placed it against the back of her knee, under her nostrils, behind her ear, in the hair under her arm. And every place my finger touched, it pressed. And everywhere it pressed, her skin resisted with the same soft strength and I thought, "This...is youth."...I lay down and buried my nose against her scalp, my nose rubbing up and down as her foot rubbed against the sheets. When I woke up, it was just past dawn. The room was bright. That's when I tried to assault her—yes, it's true, I *tried*. But I'm an honorable man, so don't worry for her. If I had known she was a virgin, I would never have even thought of it to begin with. *(Pause.)*

WOMAN. Well, this is too bad. You know the rules of the house, don't you?

KAWABATA. Yes.

WOMAN. But still...

KAWABATA. But I didn't.

WOMAN. Very technical.

KAWABATA. I don't know why. It was too bright in the room. I became sad, then angry. I wanted to hit her or something. But instead, I tried that instead.

WOMAN. Can I get you some tea?

KAWABATA. Huh? Yes, please. Thank you.

WOMAN. Why do you do that kind of thing anyway?

KAWABATA. I told you, I don't know. And don't make it sound like I do it often.

WOMAN. No, I mean about sleeping with your head in her hair.

KAWABATA. Oh, that.

WOMAN. Don't you worry about suffocating?

KAWABATA. I have my reasons.

WOMAN. Well, go on. There's very little you can't tell me now. *(Pause.)*

KAWABATA. Her hair—the girl last night. It had a special smell. Like an old lady friend of mine.

WOMAN. Your wife?

KAWABATA. No, I'm afraid not. Maybe thirty years ago. She was married to—oh, some kind of Hong Kong businessman, maybe even a movie producer—I can't remember. I do remember she lived alone with her servants—he was always away—in a huge castle in Kowloon. It really was—a castle in Kowloon. I didn't know they had castles either. Where did we meet? Kyoto? I can't—you see, I'd even forgotten her until I smelled that girl's hair. My lady friend, I'd smell her hair and she'd cry, "Don't do that. It's filthy!" But I'd smell her hair for hours. I wonder what she's doing now. She was the only woman who ever winked at me.

WOMAN. Mr. Kawabata...

KAWABATA. I was shocked. This was many years ago, you know—huh?

WOMAN. I apologize. For my hysteria.

KAWABATA. Have you...seen my point?

WOMAN. Yes.

KAWABATA. About the story? My writing?

WOMAN. Yes. Would you like to be our guest again tonight?

KAWABATA. What? Even after—?

WOMAN. I misjudged you. You are honest. That's a rare quality. I was irrational. This time, no charge. Only please stay.

KAWABATA. I came here to burn my record.

WOMAN. We can make you a new one. The girl I've picked out for you tonight is more experienced than the one before.

KAWABATA. It's not the same one?

WOMAN. No. Isn't it better to have a different one?

KAWABATA. You understand that I won't...do anything like ...last night.

WOMAN. Of course, Mr. Kawabata. I see you're a gentleman after all. Your sleeping medicine?

KAWABATA. My—Oh, thank you. I don't quite understand.

WOMAN. Don't understand. Just enjoy tonight's sleep. May I help you undress?

KAWABATA. Thank you. I suppose...I can't refuse your generosity.

WOMAN. Thank you. *(They are behind the screen.)*

KAWABATA. Uh—where was your house located before?

WOMAN. Before? We've always been here.

KAWABATA. No, but that story you told. The one about your guest the policeman.

WOMAN. Oh, that.

KAWABATA. Where did you move from?

WOMAN. We didn't. *(Pause.)* Things just worked out. *(They come out. She opens the door, gives him a key.)* Third door on your left. This one's even prettier—and more experienced.

KAWABATA. What do you mean, more experienced? After all, she's sound asleep.

WOMAN. Good night, Mr. Kawabata. *(He goes in. She closes the door. She returns to the desk, pulls out her record book, and begins to write. Lights to black.)*

Scene 3

Several months later. Kawabata, sitting alone. Silence. Woman enters from door to rooms.

WOMAN. Yes, I can arrange something tonight. *(Pause.)* But you should know better. You've been a guest for five months now. why didn't you call first, instead of just bursting in?

KAWABATA. *(Sharply.)* I'm sorry!

WOMAN. It will be a few minutes before things are ready. *(Pause.)*

KAWABATA. Can you give me some of that sleeping medicine?

WOMAN. Now? Well, if you like.

KAWABATA. No, not that. The kind you give the girls.

WOMAN. The girls?

KAWABATA. Yes. I want to sleep as deeply as they do.

WOMAN. Sir, that kind of medicine isn't healthy for old men.

KAWABATA. I can take it. I'm your guest, aren't I? You always say so. You always say you want to serve your guests, don't you?

WOMAN. What's wrong with this?

KAWABATA. I wake up. I wake up at two, three in the morning. Sometimes, it takes me an hour to fall back to sleep. I just lie there.

WOMAN. Your body shouldn't be building up resistance.

KAWABATA. That's not it.

WOMAN. If you're tired of my girls, I can arrange something special.

KAWABATA. Will it help me sleep? *(Pause.)* See? Whatever you do with the girls—it doesn't matter if I have to lie there like a stone.

WOMAN. Is there a girl here you'd like to see again?

KAWABATA. No. It's not the girls, it's me. When I began coming here, I'd lie awake at nights, too, but I'd love it, because I'd remember...things I'd forgotten for years—women, romances. I stopped writing—even exercises—it all seemed so pointless. But these last few weeks, I smell their skin, run my fingers between their toes—there's nothing there but skin and toes. I wake up in the middle of the night, and all I can remember was what it was like to remember, and I'm a prisoner in that bed.

WOMAN. I'm sorry. I can't—

KAWABATA. No. Listen. It's getting worse. Last night, when I woke up, all I could think of was the death of my friend.

WOMAN. I'm sorry.

KAWABATA. I hadn't thought of Mishima's suicide in a year. But last night—it began again—what must it have been like? *(Pause.) Hara-kiri.* How does a man you know commit *hara-kiri?* A loved one, a friend. Strangers, of course. They kill themselves daily. But someone you know—how do they find that will? *(Pause.)* The will. To feel your hands forcing steel through your stomach and if the hands stopped the pain would stop, but the hands keep going. They must become another being, your hands. Yes. Your hands become another being and the steel becomes you.

WOMAN. You shouldn't give your friend more respect than he deserves.

KAWABATA. He was a man, though. He had his lover stand behind him and chop off his head when the cutting was done.

WOMAN. I'm not going to give you dangerous drugs. I'm sorry. *(Pause.)* Don't worry so much about your friend, Mr. Kawabata. People commit suicide for themselves. That's one thing I know. I had a sister, Mr. Kawabata. My parents sent her away to Tokyo, hoping that she would be trained in the tea, the dance, the *koto*, to attract a man of wealth. I wept with envy at the fine material Mother bought for her kimonos—gold thread, brocade. The day she left, I was angry—she was crying at her good fortune. Years went by; we were both engaged. She came back from Tokyo for her wedding and we could barely recognize her—she had neither the hands nor the speech of anyone we knew. I got very angry at her haughtiness—my chore was to pick the maggots from the rice, and I purposely left a few in, hoping she would get them...Their wedding was the most beautiful I'd ever seen. Just before she was to leave, my sister cornered me outside, tears streaming down her face, and begged my forgiveness...They tried to keep the story a secret from us, but, well...such a romantic story; the stuff legends are made of. It seems my sister had a lover in the village, that they had pledged fidelity long before she left for Tokyo. The next morning, my father went to draw water from the well. In the dim light before dawn, two faces came rushing up to the water's surface. Two faces—my sister and my fiancé...So don't worry about your friend, Mr. Kawabata. People kill themselves to save themselves, not others. *(Pause.)* Now, I'm going to prepare something special. There will be two girls. There will be twice the warmth. *(She exits. He goes to the cabinet, takes out the vials and a cup. He pours and drinks three glasses of the sleeping potion. He returns the items. She reenters.)*

KAWABATA. Madame?

WOMAN. Yes.

KAWABATA. If I were to commit *hara-kiri*, would you chop off my head?

WOMAN. Mr. Kawabata—

KAWABATA. No. Answer me. If I gave you a sword—I'd pay you, you know—I wouldn't expect you to do it for nothing.

WOMAN. This type of question doesn't help either of us.

KAWABATA. Listen—would you chop off my head when I whispered, "Now. Please. Now." Or would you walk away laughing, counting your change.

WOMAN. Will you stop that? Will you stop that selfishness?

KAWABATA. No, the question is—answer it!—would you chop—

WOMAN. No! No! That's *your* question, yours only. You never think of anyone else's suffering—you're so self-centered, all you men, every last one of you. Have some woman chop off your head, leave her alone, do you think of her? She takes her few dollars, she buys some vegetables, she eats them and slowly withers away—no glory, no honor, just a slow fading into the background—that's all you expect. No. Mr. Kawabata, if *I* wanted to commit *hara-kiri*, would you chop off *my* head?

KAWABATA. Women don't commit *hara-kiri*.

WOMAN. What if I did? What if I were the first?

KAWABATA. This is pointless.

WOMAN. I know—you think I would do it the woman's way, just slipping the tiny knife in here. But what if I wanted to do it like a man? Completely. Powerfully.

KAWABATA. That's a foolish question.

WOMAN. I would do it better than you.

KAWABATA. Don't be absurd.

WOMAN. I would be braver.

KAWABATA. What a ridiculous notion!

WOMAN. If you didn't chop off my head, I'd be glad.

KAWABATA. This is a waste of time.

WOMAN. Because then, I'd be braver than you or your friend.

KAWABATA. Don't blaspheme Mishima.

WOMAN. I'd die like the generals.

KAWABATA. You're just an old woman.

WOMAN. I'd be the old woman who died like the generals.

KAWABATA. Show some respect. *(Pause.)*

WOMAN. So quiet now, aren't you, Mr. Kawabata. Why don't you spout glorious phrases about chopping off my head? *(Pause.)* Or why don't you write your report and destroy us all? *(Pause.)* Your room is ready. Should I help you undress?

KAWABATA. No. *(He starts to leave, still dressed.)*

WOMAN. Don't forget your key. *(He returns, takes the key.)*

73

Fourth door on your right. *(He exits. she closes the door. Pause. She goes to her desk, takes out a make-up kit. She stands next to the mirror, powders her face completely white, does her eyes, her mouth. She then goes to the door to the rooms, pulls up a chair, and sits facing it.)*

KAWABATA. *(Offstage.)* Madame! Madame! *(He enters, wearing only his pants. He is in a panic, but the large amount of sleeping potion he's taken has started to take effect. He stares at her. She says nothing. He is speechless. Long pause.)*

WOMAN. Go back to bed. There is still the other girl.

KAWABATA. Your...one of your girls. She's...not breathing. No pulse.

WOMAN. Her body is being removed even as you speak. Now go back to bed. There is still the other girl.

KAWABATA. Other girl?

WOMAN. Yes, there were two, remember?

KAWABATA. I can't...your face. Why is it that way? I can't go back in there. She's dead. Do something. Go in.

WOMAN. Very little I can do. She took too much of her sleeping medicine, I think.

KAWABATA. This is inhuman.

WOMAN. It's difficult, but these things happen.

KAWABATA. This is...not human.

WOMAN. Now, go back. It won't do to be walking the streets at this hour.

KAWABATA. Why do people come here? Why don't they leave? I won't...I'm leaving.

WOMAN. You can't leave.

KAWABATA. I'm leaving. Where's my shirt, my coat?

WOMAN. Where will you go?

KAWABATA. Out. Home.

WOMAN. In your condition? Look at you—what happened, anyway?

KAWABATA. No, I don't care. I'll sleep in the streets.

WOMAN. You'll die in the cold, that's what you'll do.

KAWABATA. Yes. I'll die in the cold. I'll die in the cold before I become like Old Eguchi. Look at him—pathetic—here every damn night.

74

WOMAN. Like Old Eguchi? How are you *not* like Old Eughi?

KAWABATA. I can still sleep somewhere else.

WOMAN. Today, perhaps. Tomorrow, no.

KAWABATA. Where's my shirt?

WOMAN. Here. *(She leads him to the mirror.)* Look at yourself. Even as we speak, the lines are getting deeper, the hair is getting thinner, your lips are getting drier. Even as we speak, the shape of your face is changing, and with it, a mind, a will, as different as the face. You can leave now, Mr. Kawabata, but as much as you deny it, your face will continue to change, as if your will didn't even exist. See my face? Look at it. Close. I try and powder it like a young girl. But look—all that's here is an obscene mockery of youth. Don't be like this, Mr. Kawabata. Go back to sleep and let's not hear any more of your grandstanding. *(Kawabata is firmly in the grip of the drug now.)*

KAWABATA. I'm...so tired. I drank too much of the potion.

WOMAN. That? I'm sorry. My fault. I shouldn't have left it there. Well, you should be all right. That's not as strong as the stuff you wanted.

KAWABATA. I would leave, I would, you know.

WOMAN. But you're too tired?

KAWABATA. I'm not coming back.

WOMAN. Of course not. Here. I'll help you to your room. *(She starts to sing the "Tokyo Ondo" softly as they exit together. Lights fade slowly, and we can still hear the song.)*

Scene 4

A week later. Evening. He is alone in the room. He is wrapping something in a small box. He completes the wrapping, puts the box into the breast pocket of the suit he is wearing. She enters from the door to the rooms. She carries a manuscript.

WOMAN. You've sent this to your publisher?

KAWABATA. Yes. It will be in print in time. *(Pause.)*

WOMAN. You go very easy on yourself.

KAWABATA. In what sense?

WOMAN. You don't even name the main character after yourself. You call him old Eguchi.

KAWABATA. Maybe I'm writing about him, not me.

WOMAN. And here...this story. That never happened. No man ever died here.

KAWABATA. Are you sure?

WOMAN. Who told you that?

KAWABATA. No one. I just thought...maybe.

WOMAN. And look at this. All this talk about the girls with their electric blankets. We don't even have electric blankekts.

KAWABATA. Madame, I write stories, not newspaper copy. I don't—

WOMAN. This woman—she's very...uh—she seems so hard.

KAWABATA. The story's not about her.

WOMAN. She has no feeling's no heart. She's so...above it all, like she never cries, like her heart has gone through life without stumbling. She's like a ghost that walks through men's houses without creaking the floorboards.

KAWABATA. It's rather depersonalized, objective...

WOMAN. "Objective"? How can you say that? Look at the end—here—when the girl dies—like last week—and she says, "There's still the other girl." Doesn't that make her just one kind of woman?

KAWABATA. What I mean is that—

WOMAN. Doesn't it? Yes, I said that. But I shared things with you, stories. I let you see me ridiculous, hideous, a fool in my powder. Where is that? Is this all you remember? Just an old, cruel woman who serves you tea and takes your money?

KAWABATA. You have to understand...the joy was that I could finally write again at all.

WOMAN. Yes. That is surprising.

KAWABATA. I wasn't going to stop it.

WOMAN. I was surprised we hadn't seen you all week.

KAWABATA. Do you understand?

WOMAN. Do you still think that the house will survive this story? Even after revealing the girl's death?

KAWABATA. I don't know. Who can say?

WOMAN. You didn't change anything, make it harder for them to find us.

KAWABATA. I'm sorry. I wanted to, but I couldn't. I'm sorry.

WOMAN. No. Sorry has nothing to do with it. We each do our work.

KAWABATA. When I told you last week—drugged—that I wasn't coming back again, did you believe me?

WOMAN. Of course not. But there was a part of me...Up to a point, you'd acted like all my guests. The game with the tiles, being unable to assault my girl when you found her a virgin, you fit right into the gentleman's pattern. But your memories—leaving you so soon. There was a part of me that wondered. I wanted to call you. Once I even finished dialing your number. But I hung up before it rang. I sat here and thought up tortures for you. I thought you'd gone away...committed *hara-kiri*, and that you were waiting for me to come and chop off your head. I decided to stay right here.

KAWABATA. Did you think I wasn't coming back?

WOMAN. After a time, I began to wonder. *(Pause. She goes to the mirror, looks at it.)* Well, there're many things I could do now. I could move to another city. Try to start again, from the ground. Or I could sit here, the same as always. Who knows? Perhaps no one will believe your story.

KAWABATA. That's quite possible. I've told you that.

WOMAN. Which would you recommend?

KAWABATA. Me? I don't know what kind of risks you take, or what's involved in starting over.

WOMAN. No. You don't.

KAWABATA. I think, though, that at our age, starting again is only worthwhile if one enjoys the process.

WOMAN. "At our age"?

KAWABATA. It's—uh—difficult to make long-range plans, you know.

WOMAN. Since when are we the same age?

KAWABATA. We are, aren't we?

WOMAN. Yes, we are.

KAWABATA. Give or take five years—

WOMAN. And you, then—

KAWABATA. —which hardly matters at this point.

WOMAN. —what will you do? Will you come back here?

KAWABATA. No.

WOMAN. Oh.

KAWABATA. No. My life becomes very simple now. *(He takes out a packet of bills, offers them to her.)* Here. Here. Take it. Enough for you to...I don't know, buy a new house, anywhere you want. Or retire. Yes, retire and never worry about a thing again.

WOMAN. This is...so much...amazing. I can't take this. Why?

KAWABATA. I want you to serve me.

WOMAN. This is...an outrageous amount, Mr. Kawabata. I cannot accept it.

KAWABATA. Please. You'll need the money. An even trade.

WOMAN. Do you want a girl? A room?

KAWABATA. No.

WOMAN. I can fix you something special.

KAWABATA. Fix me some tea.

WOMAN. Oh, I forgot. I'm sorry.

KAWABATA. No. Don't apologize.

WOMAN. I'm sorry. So rude of me. It's such a cold night.

KAWABATA. You make very wonderful tea.

WOMAN. No, it's not.

KAWABATA. Yes.

WOMAN. It's nothing. *(Pause.)*

KAWABATA. I've grown in this house.

WOMAN. You feel young here?

KAWABATA. I did. As I've slept here, I've grown older. I've seen my sweethearts, my wife, my mistresses, my daughters, until there's only one thing left. *(She comes with the tea.)* Will you powder

78

your face again?

WOMAN. Mr. Kawabata, don't—

KAWABATA. Please.

WOMAN. You're mocking me—an old woman.

KAWABATA. No, I've brought you something. *(He reaches into a bag he is carrying, pulls out a kimono.)*

WOMAN. Oh!

KAWABATA. Yes. Take it.

WOMAN. It's...No, this isn't for me.

KAWABATA. Yes. See? Gold thread. Brocade.

WOMAN. I can't accept this. Please. Give it to someone who deserves it.

KAWABATA. It's for you.

WOMAN. One of your young admirers. You are a famous writer. You must have many.

KAWABATA. Please. Put it on. It's just like the one you told me about.

WOMAN. It's gorgeous, too beautiful—

KAWABATA. Put it on and powder your face.

WOMAN. You're so foolish, Mr. Kawabata. I'll disgrace these clothes. Once they drape down my old bones, especially with my face in that powder, they'll change into something else completely, believe me.

KAWABATA. Don't be shy. You'll do me a great honor to wear my gift. *(Pause.)*

WOMAN. If you insist.

KAWABATA. Yes. Please. *(She starts to leave.)* No. Please. Do it here. I want to watch.

WOMAN. Women don't like men to watch them making up. *(Pause. She sits, begins making up.)*

KAWABATA. I finished that story several days ago, you know. It came out of me like a wild animal, my hands were cramping at the pen. I wanted to show it to you while it was still warm, but I kept turning back. It's the same way I've felt before when I've written the end of a story, yet known that the story had more to do before I could rest. So I trusted my instincts—I watched television for two full days, since usually, what hasn't yet been revealed will rise to the surface in its own time. Yesterday, I woke up and knew what had to be added, and words weren't the question at all, so I sent the manuscript as it was to my publisher and went out shopping.

WOMAN. For the kimono? It's so beautiful.

KAWABATA. I tried to imagine the one you described.

WOMAN. This is every bit as beautiful.

KAWABATA. It's not the same?

WOMAN. It's difficult for me to remember. I was so young. But my sister's couldn't have been any finer. *(She takes the kimono, goes behind the screen, begins changing into it. He takes the small box out of his breast pocket, removes his jacket, takes off his tie, unbuttons his collar, takes off his shoes. Finally, she speaks.)* After the war, when we realized Father wasn't coming back, and the family was dispersed, I moved here to Tokyo. And I thought, "Now I'll dress in brocade also. I'll wear gold threads, too." But when I remembered my sister, I lost any desire to have anything like that. It's just as well, that being after the war and all. And I've never had the money, even to this day—ai! You'd think at my age, I'd have earned the right to stop worrying about money.

KAWABATA. But I've given you your security.

WOMAN. Yes, yes. I still can't—But why? *(She steps out from behind the screen.)* See? Don't I look hideous?

KAWABATA. You're exactly what I want.

WOMAN. Is this what you want? An old hag pretending to be young again?

KAWABATA. Please. Sit down.

WOMAN. The tea—it's probably cold.

KAWABATA. No, it's fine. open that box.

WOMAN. This one?

KAWABATA. Yes.

WOMAN. It's beautifully wrapped. *(She starts to open it.)*

KAWABATA. It took me several hours to buy the kimono, and the rest of the day to buy that. *(She removes a vial of clear liquid.)* Please. Add it to the tea. *(Pause.)* Go on. You said it was all right for us to bring our own medicine, didn't you? *(Pause.)* The top lifts off.

(Pause.) Don't worry. I'm not going to ask you to drink it or anything. It's for me. Now, go on.

WOMAN. Respect me, Mr. Kawabata.

KAWABATA. I do.

WOMAN. Tell me—this isn't a sleeping potion.

KAWABATA. No.

WOMAN. Do you want a room?

KAWABATA. No.

WOMAN. I want to give you one. Free.

KAWABATA. I've already paid.

WOMAN. For what?

KAWABATA. Paid not to have a room.

WOMAN. For me?

KAWABATA. Please, empty the vial.

WOMAN. No. *(Pause.)*

KAWABATA. Isn't this your job? Isn't this what you get paid to do? For your life's security, madame, you should be willing to endure a little more than usual. *(Pause.)* What's the matter? I thought of all people in the world, you would understand this. *(Silence. She empties the vial into the pot.)* Good. I'm sorry. I didn't mean to do that, say those things. But I assume...we have an understanding. Do we?

WOMAN. Look at me. See this? *(Her face.)* This? *(Her dress.)* That should answer your question. What should I do now?

KAWABATA. Tell me again, why I should come to your house.

WOMAN. *(As before.)* Our guests sleep very well here. It's the warmth, they say.

KAWABATA. Warmth?

WOMAN. Our guests are not afraid to sleep at night. The darkness does not threaten them.

KAWABATA. Oh, it's so cold tonight. Look at my hand. Could you pour me some tea, please? *(Pause.)*

WOMAN. Yes. Certainly. *(She does; her eyes are fixed on him. She watches him drink as she speaks.)* The girl I've picked out for you is...she's...half Japanese, half caucasian, very beautiful, like a child, like a pearly-white snowflake child, whose foot never—always—moves, traces circles around the snow—uh—sheet, fleeing—uh—feeling the warmth, the heart—uh—the heat, finding it, the warmth, the heart—uh—the heat, taking it, the warmth, the heat, always... *(He puts down the cup. It is empty. Pause. She refills his cup. It sits on the table, untouched. Silence.)*

KAWABATA. Now, we are as we should be.

WOMAN. Yes, I suppose so.

KAWABATA. And you look so beautiful.

WOMAN. Don't be cruel.

KAWABATA. But you do.

WOMAN. I won't listen.

KAWABATA. If we were thirty, maybe even twenty years younger, who knows?

WOMAN. Mr. Kawabata, for so long now, you've been trying to show me that you're different from my other guests.

KAWABATA. I'm sorry.

WOMAN. No, no, you've done it. You've gotten your wish. How does it make you feel?

KAWABATA. I wasted so much time.

WOMAN. You've proven to me that you're a thousand times more terrible and wonderful than any of my other guests.

KAWABATA. How sad. I don't even care about that anymore. If I'm different, it's only because I believed you when you showed me that I was the same as the rest of them. *(Pause.)* It's funny. I've known you all this time, and I don't even know your name.

WOMAN. Michiko.

KAWABATA. Michiko. Wonderful. You have the hands of a young woman, did you know that, Michiko?

WOMAN. No. My hands are ugly.

KAWABATA. Let me see them, Michiko.

WOMAN. They are the hands of a crow.

KAWABATA. Please. Let me see them. *(She does.)* Amazing. And you—from the country. *(He touches them.)* They are long. And firm. And warm with blood. *(He kisses them.)* I'm starting to become tired. May I rest in your lap? *(She nods.)* Thank you, Michiko.

(Silently, she begins to stroke his hair.) You've been very kind for allowing me to...take these liberties with you. I'm sorry I said those things about you. But I was afraid that you weren't as strong as I expected, that you couldn't give me what I needed. I shouldn't have doubted. *(Pause.)* Please. Take the money. Be happy. Enjoy these last years. Buy what you've always wanted. *(Pause.)* I do want you to take care of yourself. *(Silence.)* You can't believe what a comfort it is for me to be falling asleep, yet able to open my eyes, look up, and see you. *(His eyes are closed. She looks around the house, continues to stroke his hair. She begins to sing the "Tokyo Ondo" as a lullaby. She picks up the remaining cup of tea, drinks it. She resumes singing, strokes his hair, as lights fade to black.)*

CURTAIN

PROPERTY LIST

SCENE 1
Desk, with make-up kit in drawer
Pillows
Low table
Tea service
Cabinet, with vial & cups
Screen
Mirror
Wood burning furnace
Pen & pencil
Box of tiles, in desk
Small jar of liquid & cup
Robe

SCENE 2
Key
Record book, in desk

SCENE 4
Small box, with vial of clear liquid
Wrapping paper
Manuscript
Packet of bills (Kawabata)
Tea service
Bag, with kimono

NEW PLAYS

★ **MONTHS ON END by Craig Pospisil.** In comic scenes, one for each month of the year, we follow the intertwined worlds of a circle of friends and family whose lives are poised between happiness and heartbreak. "...a triumph...these twelve vignettes all form crucial pieces in the eternal puzzle known as human relationships, an area in which the playwright displays an assured knowledge that spans deep sorrow to unbounded happiness." *–Ann Arbor News.* "...rings with emotional truth, humor...[an] endearing contemplation on love...entertaining and satisfying." *–Oakland Press.* [5M, 5W] ISBN: 0-8222-1892-5

★ **GOOD THING by Jessica Goldberg.** Brings us into the households of John and Nancy Roy, forty-something high-school guidance counselors whose marriage has been increasingly on the rocks and Dean and Mary, recent graduates struggling to make their way in life. "...a blend of gritty social drama, poetic humor and unsubtle existential contemplation..." *–Variety.* [3M, 3W] ISBN: 0-8222-1869-0

★ **THE DEAD EYE BOY by Angus MacLachlan.** Having fallen in love at their Narcotics Anonymous meeting, Billy and Shirley-Diane are striving to overcome the past together. But their relationship is complicated by the presence of Sorin, Shirley-Diane's fourteen-year-old son, a damaged reminder of her dark past. "...a grim, insightful portrait of an unmoored family..." *–NY Times.* "MacLachlan's play isn't for the squeamish, but then, tragic stories delivered at such an unrelenting fever pitch rarely are." *–Variety.* [1M, 1W, 1 boy] ISBN: 0-8222-1844-5

★ **[SIC] by Melissa James Gibson.** In adjacent apartments three young, ambitious neighbors come together to discuss, flirt, argue, share their dreams and plan their futures with unequal degrees of deep hopefulness and abject despair. "A work...concerned with the sound and power of language..." *–NY Times.* "...a wonderfully original take on urban friendship and the comedy of manners—a *Design for Living* for our times..." *–NY Observer.* [3M, 2W] ISBN: 0-8222-1872-0

★ **LOOKING FOR NORMAL by Jane Anderson.** Roy and Irma's twenty-five-year marriage is thrown into turmoil when Roy confesses that he is actually a woman trapped in a man's body, forcing the couple to wrestle with the meaning of their marriage and the delicate dynamics of family. "Jane Anderson's bittersweet transgender domestic comedy-drama ...is thoughtful and touching and full of wit and wisdom. A real audience pleaser." *–Hollywood Reporter.* [5M, 4W] ISBN: 0-8222-1857-7

★ **ENDPAPERS by Thomas McCormack.** The regal Joshua Maynard, the old and ailing head of a mid-sized, family-owned book-publishing house in New York City, must name a successor. One faction in the house backs a smart, "pragmatic" manager, the other faction a smart, "sensitive" editor and both factions fear what the other's man could do to this house— and to them. "If Kaufman and Hart had undertaken a comedy about the publishing business, they might have written *Endpapers*...a breathlessly fast, funny, and thoughtful comedy ...keeps you amused, guessing, and often surprised...profound in its empathy for the paradoxes of human nature." *–NY Magazine.* [7M, 4W] ISBN: 0-8222-1908-5

★ **THE PAVILION by Craig Wright.** By turns poetic and comic, romantic and philosophical, this play asks old lovers to face the consequences of difficult choices made long ago. "The script's greatest strength lies in the genuineness of its feeling." *–Houston Chronicle.* "Wright's perceptive, gently witty writing makes this familiar situation fresh and thoroughly involving." *–Philadelphia Inquirer.* [2M, 1W (flexible casting)] ISBN: 0-8222-1898-4

DRAMATISTS PLAY SERVICE, INC.
440 Park Avenue South, New York, NY 10016 212-683-8960 Fax 212-213-1539
postmaster@dramatists.com www.dramatists.com

NEW PLAYS

★ **BE AGGRESSIVE by Annie Weisman.** Vista Del Sol is paradise, sandy beaches, avocado-lined streets. But for seventeen-year-old cheerleader Laura, everything changes when her mother is killed in a car crash, and she embarks on a journey to the Spirit Institute of the South where she can learn "cheer" with Bible belt intensity. "...filled with lingual gymnastics...stylized rapid-fire dialogue..." *–Variety.* "...a new, exciting, and unique voice in the American theatre..." *–BackStage West.* [1M, 4W, extras] ISBN: 0-8222-1894-1

★ **FOUR by Christopher Shinn.** Four people struggle desperately to connect in this quiet, sophisticated, moving drama. "...smart, broken-hearted...Mr. Shinn has a precocious and forgiving sense of how power shifts in the game of sexual pursuit...He promises to be a playwright to reckon with..." *–NY Times.* "A voice emerges from an American place. It's got humor, sadness and a fresh and touching rhythm that tell of the loneliness and secrets of life...[a] poetic, haunting play." *–NY Post.* [3M, 1W] ISBN: 0-8222-1850-X

★ **WONDER OF THE WORLD by David Lindsay-Abaire.** A madcap picaresque involving Niagara Falls, a lonely tour-boat captain, a pair of bickering private detectives and a husband's dirty little secret. "Exceedingly whimsical and playfully wicked. Winning and genial. A top-drawer production." *–NY Times.* "Full frontal lunacy is on display. A most assuredly fresh and hilarious tragicomedy of marital discord run amok...absolutely hysterical..." *–Variety.* [3M, 4W (doubling)] ISBN: 0-8222-1863-1

★ **QED by Peter Parnell.** Nobel Prize-winning physicist and all-around genius Richard Feynman holds forth with captivating wit and wisdom in this fascinating biographical play that originally starred Alan Alda. "QED is a seductive mix of science, human affections, moral courage, and comic eccentricity. It reflects on, among other things, death, the absence of God, travel to an unexplored country, the pleasures of drumming, and the need to know and understand." *–NY Magazine.* "Its rhythms correspond to the way that people—even geniuses—approach and avoid highly emotional issues, and it portrays Feynman with affection and awe." *–The New Yorker.* [1M, 1W] ISBN: 0-8222-1924-7

★ **UNWRAP YOUR CANDY by Doug Wright.** Alternately chilling and hilarious, this deliciously macabre collection of four bedtime tales for adults is guaranteed to keep you awake for nights on end. "Engaging and intellectually satisfying...a treat to watch." *–NY Times.* "Fiendishly clever. Mordantly funny and chilling. Doug Wright teases, freezes and zaps us." *–Village Voice.* "Four bite-size plays that bite back." *–Variety.* [flexible casting] ISBN: 0-8222-1871-2

★ **FURTHER THAN THE FURTHEST THING by Zinnie Harris.** On a remote island in the middle of the Atlantic secrets are buried. When the outside world comes calling, the islanders find their world blown apart from the inside as well as beyond. "Harris winningly produces an intimate and poetic, as well as political, family saga." *–Independent (London).* "Harris' enthralling adventure of a play marks a departure from stale, well-furrowed theatrical terrain." *–Evening Standard (London).* [3M, 2W] ISBN: 0-8222-1874-7

★ **THE DESIGNATED MOURNER by Wallace Shawn.** The story of three people living in a country where what sort of books people like to read and how they choose to amuse themselves becomes both firmly personal and unexpectedly entangled with questions of survival. "This is a playwright who does not just tell you what it is like to be arrested at night by goons or to fall morally apart and become an aimless yet weirdly contented ghost yourself. He has the originality to make you feel it." *–Times (London).* "A fascinating play with beautiful passages of writing..." *–Variety.* [2M, 1W] ISBN: 0-8222-1848-8

DRAMATISTS PLAY SERVICE, INC.
440 Park Avenue South, New York, NY 10016 212-683-8960 Fax 212-213-1539
postmaster@dramatists.com www.dramatists.com

NEW PLAYS

★ **SHEL'S SHORTS by Shel Silverstein.** Lauded poet, songwriter and author of children's books, the incomparable Shel Silverstein's short plays are deeply infused with the same wicked sense of humor that made him famous. "...[a] childlike honesty and twisted sense of humor." –*Boston Herald.* "...terse dialogue and an absurdity laced with a tang of dread give [*Shel's Shorts*] more than a trace of Samuel Beckett's comic existentialism." –*Boston Phoenix.* [flexible casting] ISBN: 0-8222-1897-6

★ **AN ADULT EVENING OF SHEL SILVERSTEIN by Shel Silverstein.** Welcome to the darkly comic world of Shel Silverstein, a world where nothing is as it seems and where the most innocent conversation can turn menacing in an instant. These ten imaginative plays vary widely in content, but the style is unmistakable. "...[*An Adult Evening*] shows off Silverstein's virtuosic gift for wordplay...[and] sends the audience out...with a clear appreciation of human nature as perverse and laughable." –*NY Times.* [flexible casting] ISBN: 0-8222-1873-9

★ **WHERE'S MY MONEY? by John Patrick Shanley.** A caustic and sardonic vivisection of the institution of marriage, laced with the author's inimitable razor-sharp wit. "...Shanley's gift for acid-laced one-liners and emotionally tumescent exchanges is certainly potent..." –*Variety.* "...lively, smart, occasionally scary and rich in reverse wisdom." –*NY Times.* [3M, 3W] ISBN: 0-8222-1865-8

★ **A FEW STOUT INDIVIDUALS by John Guare.** A wonderfully screwy comedy-drama that figures Ulysses S. Grant in the throes of writing his memoirs, surrounded by a cast of fantastical characters, including the Emperor and Empress of Japan, the opera star Adelina Patti and Mark Twain. "Guare's smarts, passion and creativity skyrocket to awesome heights..." –*Star Ledger.* "...precisely the kind of good new play that you might call an everyday miracle...every minute of it is fresh and newly alive..." –*Village Voice.* [10M, 3W] ISBN: 0-8222-1907-7

★ **BREATH, BOOM by Kia Corthron.** A look at fourteen years in the life of Prix, a Bronx native, from her ruthless girl-gang leadership at sixteen through her coming to maturity at thirty. "...vivid world, believable and eye-opening, a place worthy of a dramatic visit, where no one would want to live but many have to." –*NY Times.* "...rich with humor, terse vernacular strength and gritty detail..." –*Variety.* [1M, 9W] ISBN: 0-8222-1849-6

★ **THE LATE HENRY MOSS by Sam Shepard.** Two antagonistic brothers, Ray and Earl, are brought together after their father, Henry Moss, is found dead in his seedy New Mexico home in this classic Shepard tale. "...His singular gift has been for building mysteries out of the ordinary ingredients of American family life..." –*NY Times.* "...rich moments ...Shepard finds gold." –*LA Times.* [7M, 1W] ISBN: 0-8222-1858-5

★ **THE CARPETBAGGER'S CHILDREN by Horton Foote.** One family's history spanning from the Civil War to WWII is recounted by three sisters in evocative, intertwining monologues. "...bittersweet music—[a] rhapsody of ambivalence...in its modest, garrulous way...theatrically daring." –*The New Yorker.* [3W] ISBN: 0-8222-1843-7

★ **THE NINA VARIATIONS by Steven Dietz.** In this funny, fierce and heartbreaking homage to *The Seagull*, Dietz puts Chekhov's star-crossed lovers in a room and doesn't let them out. "A perfect little jewel of a play..." –*Shepherdstown Chronicle.* "...a delightful revelation of a writer at play; and also an odd, haunting, moving theater piece of lingering beauty." –*Eastside Journal (Seattle).* [1M, 1W (flexible casting)] ISBN: 0-8222-1891-7

DRAMATISTS PLAY SERVICE, INC.
440 Park Avenue South, New York, NY 10016 212-683-8960 Fax 212-213-1539
postmaster@dramatists.com www.dramatists.com